Life is Hard

Soften It with Laughter

Marlene Ratledge Buchanan

TURNIP PRESS PUBLISHING — MONROE, GEORGIA

Life is Hard Soften it with Laughter

Copyright © Marlene Ratledge Buchanan 2018

All characters in this book, are fictitious. Any resemblance to actual persons, living or dead, is purely coincidental.

All rights reserved

Turnip Press Publishing
ATTN: Rights and Permissions Department
525 Michael Circle
Monroe, Georgia 30655
Email: turnippresspub@gmail.com
First Printing November16, 2018

US ISBN 978-0-9982811-3-1

Asking for forgiveness.

After numerous reading and re-writing of this material, I can promise you there will be mistakes. I tried. I really did. I am only human, and Hissy Prissy hates me. You will meet my computer, Hissy Prissy, later and will understand that she can and will do weird things with spacing and spelling if she is in one of her moods.

Disclaimer

Any similarity to anyone, living or dead, in this book is a coincidence, and all the characters in these essays are fictional. This is my life. These are my people. So be it. Some names have been changed to protect the inept.

Dedication

Snell: The tears and laughter of every word of this book were shared with my husband Snell. I knew the night we had our first date that he was my soul mate. I thought about getting HIM pregnant, so he would marry me, but after asking him three times he finally gave in and accepted my proposal. He has made such a difference in the lives of so many people, especially in mine and my parents. I love you.

James: Thinking we would never have a baby, we were stunned after seven years of marriage to learn we were pregnant. Yes, WE were pregnant. Snell hung in there with every ache, pain, and all the days of morning sickness, which began fifteen minutes after conception and lasted at least fifteen days after the baby's birth. After a difficult delivery, our beautiful baby boy, James Scott, came into this world.   Being deprived of oxygen resulted in him being mildly mentally handicapped. He is not special needs. He is a special gift.

Mama and Daddy: In memory of my parents, James Edward Ratledge and Grace Evans Ratledge. For better or worse, they made me, guided me, let me make mistakes, picked me up, and dusted me off. I miss you both every day.

Dear Reader,

Enjoy and thank you. I do appreciate you reading my essays. Without you, there would have been no point to this collection. I hope you find it lightens your day.

Life is hard. Soften it with laughter,

Marlene Ratledge Buchanan

Table of Contents

400 Words or Less

Relationships

Home and Life

Other Side of Laughter

Cats

Health

Nature

Fashion and Travel

Southern Musing

400 Words or Less

Express myself in 400 words or less?

Impossible!

400 Words or Less

I have a real problem. I have just been told to limit my columns to 400 words. Yep, you read that right— 400 words. You know me? Have we ever had a conversation of 400 words or less? No, I didn't think so either.

I can't say hello in 400 words. And if I know you and your family, 400 words is not enough for a minimum greeting. I mean, it doesn't even make a drop in the bucket. It takes me 400 words to describe spitting into the bucket, and then I have to describe the bucket.

For example, if I see you in a restaurant, I begin with, "Hey, Y'all. How are you doing? How's your mama and daddy? I haven't seen you since so- and-so died." (Funerals are one of our most important social activities.) Have you seen so-and-so? What in the world have you been doing? You are looking so good. I like that shirt, necklace, pin, nail polish, hair, etc. I saw your grandparents/aunt/cousin/friend/classmate/former boyfriend/ex-husband the other day. Did you hear about such-and-such happening?" Now, after we have done a basic greeting, we spend time catching up on all the people we know and about events. Of course, we have to spend a few minutes re-living our earlier times together. Finally, after 400 words or more, I move on, saying, "When you get a chance, y'all come see us."

Now, we all go our separate ways to eat our meals, but before leaving the restaurant, we say good bye to each other. I can maybe say good bye in 400 words. Maybe. Maybe not. "It was so good to see you. We are glad you are doing well (or sorry you are not doing well.) When you get a chance, just give us a call or come see us. You know where we are, and there is always a shovel by the back door, so you can make your way in. You are always welcome. Tell your grandmama/kids/cousins/fellow classmates/relatives and various acquaintances that we said hey. Y'all come. Hugs, everybody." That might be the end, unless we start on another conversation, or someone else we know walks up.

So. Shut my mouth after 400 words? Limit my descriptions? It is going to be a challenge. I admit it. I don't start out with an outline; I just write to you like I talk. My monthly "Hey Y'all" column may have to come in two or three installments. You may have to call me, so we can finish it up.

Well, I really haven't done anything but tell you I can't do it in 400 words. Maybe I can. We'll see. Bye, y'all. (Dang, 449 words.)

Laughter and Shopping

One of my dearest friends is an evil influence on me. Not to say that I might tempt him into a very good, but expensive decision, as well. Keith Rex is a funny, handsome fellow who agrees with me that gaudy is not just a fashion statement, but an important state of mind. Together, we can take gaudy to a new level.

His favorite colors are various shades of orange and yellow. Mine are yellow, purple, and most anything else, except brown. We dress to impress. The impression we give might not be a favorable impression, but it is impressive. No, really, we dress in business appropriate clothing, but we might glitter a little more than most.

I never laugh as much as I do with Keith. I never spend as much money, either. Keith owns J & K Fleas An'Tiques (pronounced fleasandticks quickly or flea and ticks slowly in a pronounced Southern drawl.) and the Junque Korner in Madison, Georgia. He also has another large antique and neat stuff mall in Gray, Georgia. The three are wonderful stores full of all kinds of treasures.

When Keith and I are together, we have the best time. Unfortunately, our time together usually includes spending money. I went to the Atlanta Merchandise Mart with Keith last week, and I bought my anniversary, Christmas, Hanukkah, Easter, and birthday presents possibly for the next two years... a ring and a bracelet, neither of which did I need. I am blaming Keith. He is blaming me for making him buy things. So, our relationship is a win-win situation.

We start our day having breakfast at our favorite bacon trough, Baby Jane's in Snellville. All you can eat bacon and all the other breakfast foods you want. Bacon grease is the best way we know to glide through life.

I have to be sure Keith is well fed at breakfast. He accuses me of starving him while we are on the hunt. I do bring him gluten free cardboard energy bars and water, but you use all your energy in trying to chew them. One time, he brought himself a peanut butter and jelly sandwich and a Mountain Dew. At least, what I feed him will kill him more slowly.

We spend the next five or six hours on our feet. I rarely wear much jewelry when we shop because I am always wearing his while he searches through trays of rings and other items. He has a very successful antique and unique jewelry business. The newer items that he finds at the Mart are also a lucrative part of the business. Who knew skulls and the Grim Reaper were as popular as crosses and angels? Actually, thinking back to my college days, I used to draw a lot of hoo-doody Grim Reaper pictures and sell them.

All the time we are there, we are laughing. We flirt with the people. We pick at each other. We make conversation, and we laugh some more. Someone asked if I was his mother. Well, that wasn't quite as funny as some things that are asked of us. Then I thought, I would be proud to be his mother. Of course, I am much too young, MUCH too young. Did you see that? MUCH too young. I just look old and aged. Maybe it is because Keith looks so young and perky. Anyway, I liked it better when people used to ask if we were married.

Want to spend an enjoyable day shopping and exploring interesting things? Go down to Madison to Keith's J&K Flea –n-tiques or the Junque Korner. You will find some interesting and enticing things and some beautiful things like my son's glass blown items (hint, hint). You will know many of the items were chosen by two of the best hyena-laughing friends in the world.

The Sicky Ickies

It is fall, and the kids are back at school, sharing the sicky-ickies. This term may not be in the medical books, but parents and teachers the world over know what it means.

Snell and I have been retired for years, but school has started, and we automatically succumb to the first term sicky-ickies. Snell woke up the other morning sniffling and feeling crappy. He went to the doctor who told him he had an allergy and to take an over the counter allergy medication. Three days later I woke up with his "allergy." Sorry, Doc. I think you misdiagnosed this one. It was definitely the fall semester sickie-ickies. Retired or not, our bodies automatically know the season and surrender to the dreaded, annual ailments.

At the beginning of each school year when the students were sharing germs Snell would have a little cold/allergy. At least once a year, I would catch something from one the kids at school or through my own kid at home. The sicky-ickies are the perils of working in the school system. The first two years, all new teachers should receive extra sick days. They catch everything that comes around.

I think childhood viruses spend the summer mutating so that new strains start the school year. When you were a kid, were you sick a lot during the first term of school? I bet you, your parents, and your teachers were.

The children would be sick for one or two days. The teachers would be sick for a week and still come to school. They really didn't come for the love of teaching or to spread the joy of sickness. They came because they couldn't get a sub during the first term of school. They were either already working for someone else with the sickie-ickies or ill with the new virus/flu/whatever they caught from subbing the week before.

I went from kindergarten through graduate school and never missed a day. Yep, that's eighteen years with no absences. I didn't even get a recognition when I graduated from high school. I had the measles, the mumps, and the chicken pox as a child. I was lucky, I guess, for I was always sick at either Christmas or Easter break. Sick as a dog, but the day school was back in session, I would be well enough to return.

All new teachers should be warned about the first term sickie ickies. I got sick the first term I taught. I couldn't believe it. Eighteen years of perfect attendance, and wham! I got the flu of the moment.

We used to tell parents that winter break was the salvation to the epidemics of first semester. It broke all the cycles of the random illnesses. Second semester, mono flared up. Spring break helped with this illness. Now, we need to address how after several years of retirement the dreaded sicky-ickies had found their way to our retired teachers' household. I don't know what sicky-ickie person shared this mess with Snell. I don't appreciate it. It has been three days. He has yet to feel better and has shared the sicky-ickies with me.

When I get a sicky-ickie, it crawls right to my bronchial tubes and begins multiplying. Within hours my bronchial tubes start to panic causing shortness of breath. The little tubules in my lungs start to play a death rattle. Right now, I am wheezing the 1812 Overture. When time comes for the cannon to fire, I cough up a lung.

Y'all be careful of the first term sicky-ickies. They are out to get you. I gotta go blow my nose—again.

Charm Bracelets

When I was sixteen, Mama and Daddy gave me a silver charm bracelet loaded with charms that represented my high school. Later, every time we visited another state, Daddy bought me another charm as a memento of our trip. It now must weigh a pound, maybe more. I probably should have sold it when silver was bringing such a high price, but who can sell memories like that?

I now wear another charm bracelet. Daddy was a big man and wore a size thirteen wedding ring. He had several Masonic rings as well. When Daddy died, those things went into Mama's jewelry box, and there they stayed until she was reunited with him.

I am an only child. Mama left me a notebook filled with all the information I needed in order to handle her affairs. In it, she told me to do whatever I wanted with her's and Daddy's jewelry. She knew no one else could wear Daddy's rings. I pondered what to do with them for a long time.

I knew I didn't want to melt their jewelry down into just something else. I really didn't want to get rid of their things at all. My husband, Snell, mentioned that maybe I should have one of Mama's or Daddy's rings made into a pendant for a necklace. Then it hit me. CHARMS!

I had the heads of all their rings cut off and made into charms. I have a tennis bracelet that had gold loops as part of the design. The charms hung perfectly from those links. I am not usually much of a bracelet

9

person, so I had rarely worn that tennis bracelet up to this time. It certainly gets worn now.

I had Daddy's wedding ring made smaller so that I can wear it on my thumb, together with wedding rings that had belonged to his mother and my aunt. I added a band I had bought for my husband when we thought his wedding band was lost.

I wear Mama's engagement and wedding bands on my pinkie finger. On the charm bracelet itself are the heads of Daddy's Masonic ring and Mama's Eastern Star ring. I have added Snell's baby ring, a pearl drop from my baby pictures with my parents, the first pendant Snell ever gave me, the head of my Rainbow Girls ring, and a small, gold rat from a pin I had given Mama. Ratledge is my maiden name.

The one other item of their jewelry that everyone asks me about is an odd-shaped key. On one side of that old key is raised lettering of "L.Hart/160/ Victoria /Victoria Station." On the other side in matching print is "Watch Maker & Jewelers." It is the winding key to a watch. You may have noticed that really old clocks and pocket watches must be wound with a key instead of by the stem. That key fits an 1850's Lady Hunter's watch that Daddy sent home to Mama during World War II. She wore it as a broach; I wear it as a pendant,

I do wear my charm bracelet quite a bit. I just look at the different items and think fond thoughts. I don't know that I would call it a "lucky charm bracelet," but certainly it brings me lovely memories.

Pickle and Christmas

As a child, my best friend Dotti, AKA Pickle, lived next door. We both shared the common bond of being the only child in our households. Every Christmas, we made elaborate plans about how we were going to call each other during the night when we discovered what Santa Claus had brought. Of course, we never did because we usually slept through the night. It never dawned on us that one of our parents would answer the phone.

We both anticipated the Sears Christmas catalogue each year. The day it arrived in the mail, we spent hours looking through the pages and picking out everything we wanted. That poor old catalog was pretty tattered by the time Christmas arrived, but it had provided many hours of fun and dreams. Between the two of us, our wish lists value probably rivaled the contents of Fort Knox.

We did not receive everything or the most expensive item on our wish lists. But Santa Claus always managed to place at least one item from our list under the tree. One year, I wished for a Lotus Blossom doll. She had articulated joints at her hands, elbows, knees, and ankles. She wore a pale pink "oriental style" pants and top. She was beautiful. I still have her, but sadly all her lovely clothes have been lost.

There was the year Dotti and I got bicycles and we rode in circles on the patio. Pickle got a life size toddler doll one year. Scared the devil out of you when you walked into her room.

11

Of course, most of Christmas day would be spent with our families. However, we did manage to have that phone conversation, spilling all the information about what Santa left us. We would have to wait for the day after Christmas to be able to get together and compare our loot.

Another one of my cherished memories of Christmas and Pickle was her daddy and their Christmas tree. We had an aluminum tree with the multi-color light wheel. Pickle and her family always had a fresh green tree. Pickle's daddy, Fred, was a gifted baker and made the most wonderful desserts. Between the smell of the tree and her father's cakes, their home always had the fragrance of Christmas. That was another part of Christmas at Pickles' home I loved. Fred's desserts and sweets.

Time has passed. Life has carried Pickle and me in different directions, but we have managed to stay in touch. Every Christmas, I pull the old aluminum tree of my childhood from storage. I'd love to find another one. Our tree could use a little help to be fluffy again with additional branches. That old tree becomes a time machine for me with its original twirling light transporting me to the days when Pickle and I shared more than the pages of a Sears Christmas catalogue between us.

Take Cover We are at War

Well, okay, it turns out we weren't exactly at war, but it sure sounded that way. It was early one Sunday morning when gunshots start going off in our basement. We were all sound asleep. My Daddy was a detective for the City of Atlanta School and Police Departments. He met my dates with a Smith & Wesson .38 holstered on his hip. I grew up thinking that it was normal to have a 6'4" man wearing a gun everywhere we went. Maybe most people didn't, but I did.

Daddy had a call that had taken him out during the night, and I don't think he had returned until around four or five in the morning. We were all blissfully asleep when the first shot sounded around six a.m. I think that is what woke me up. I know I was awake by the next couple of blasts. I ran to the basement door calling Puddles, our dog. Thankfully, Puddles was upstairs and not in the range of the gun fire.

Daddy came running down the hall in his T-shirt, Jockey shorts, and a .38. Mama was behind him saying "What is that? I've got the shotgun." Mama grew up on a farm. She could handle any firearm you gave her.   I believe I was thinking, "Why don't I have a gun?"

In his loudest voice, Puddles was saying "Let me at 'em. I'll take care of my family".

About the time Daddy hit the turn in the steps going to the basement, a volley of shots rang out. And the stench. OH Lord, what had been killed in the basement

13

and how long ago had it died? Even Puddles looked back like "What me? I might roll around in dead stuff, but this is just too awful!"

Back in the summer, Mama had canned and frozen a lot of vegetables. One of our favorite things was her homemade vegetable soup. It had tomatoes, corn, cabbage, butterbeans, and some other vegetables. Apparently, the butterbeans fermented, and they exploded. Yes, thirty-four mason jars of vegetable soup had assaulted my family that peaceful morning.

Relationships

"My plans were to marry a rich old man. I only got old. Snell is eleven years my senior, but I wouldn't trade him for anything. Mainly, because I don't want to train another one!"

Destiny

D o you believe in destiny? I believe in a lot of things. I believe in ghosts, eeni-meanie mini-moe, and destiny. I married my husband 364 days after our first date. That was, however, four years after we first met. Apparently, being twenty-two years old and wearing a mini-skirt as short as I could get it and hair longer than the skirt itself was not too impressive. I thought I was pretty cute. He thought I was jail bait.

My husband's name is William Snell Buchanan. Everyone calls him by his middle name, which is his mother's maiden name. Male children frequently get their mother's maiden name for their first or middle names. William is his daddy's name. Snell's brother, Jimmy, was given their father's middle name-- Erskine. Not sure who won out in the name game here. Like Snell said, growing up in Snellville and every third person was a Snell, no one paid his name any mind. It is the foreigners (those people not of Snellville) who always ask him about his name. He usually introduces himself as William to new people. Then I slip up and call him Snell, and he still has to explain his name.

But this is off task. I was asked to write about our romance. Romance is not my forte'. I write with humor about life, death and destruction. The idea of throwing a headless body into this story telling is tempting. Please hang in here with me.

At the time we first met, Snell and I were both educators in the fastest growing county in the United States. I was an art teacher at Duluth High School on the northern side of the county, and he was a counselor at South Gwinnett High School on the southern side of the school district. I was asked to go to a meeting on testing for my school, and Snell was there. A mutual friend named Frances introduced us in the hallway.

At the age of twenty-two, I thought I was fetching to the opposite sex. My ta-tas stood at attention. I had a teeny waist, wore high heels, and was able to jump over a cafeteria table in a single bound. My teaching career was under six months old in comparison to Snell's ten years. Not only did he have years of experience as a teacher over me, Snell was ten and half years my senior. Yeah, a little difference.

He thought I was a student teacher when we were introduced. He smiled, shook my hand, and said something like "nice to meet you." He turned to Frances, the woman I was with, and started talking about business and other things. Okay. I did not impress him. I went on into the room and took a hundred pages of notes on how to give tests to our poor students.

Speed through four years. I was twenty-six and apparently not quite as off putting to Snell. Teaching must have been hard on me because I had lost the jail bait glow. We were giving tests to determine which students would be selected to participate in the Georgia Department of Education sponsored summer experience, the Governor's Honors Program. I was to give the foreign language exams.

Yep, wrong subject for me! I was cussing the tape recorder because it hated me and wouldn't talk in French. It was just whirring and purring and being obnoxious. Finally, someone came in, pushed one button, and the thing started bonjouring and oui-ouing all over the place.

We had a little break from the testing and had gathered in the lobby area. Everyone was talking about different things and introducing ourselves to each other. Snell walked up with some other teachers.

How is this for an opening? "What do you do in Snellville besides watch the one traffic light change?" Well, I was still a bit flustered with the damn tape recorder. He just laughed. Later, he told me he thought I was a cute as a speckled pup. Really? A dog? Well, he did say pup. Puppies are cute. He also confessed during our first year of dating he thought I was not only too young, but WAY too young.

One of the assistant principals at my school was trying to fix Snell up with my best friend, Sharon who was big into sports. She kept the game record books, sponsored cheerleading, and knew all about the rules and regulations of football, baseball and basketball. Snell coached football and track and filmed the games. I went to almost all of the ball games, too. I sold tickets and then visited with everyone in the stands. My knowledge of sports could be summed up into what our son said when he described football when he was about five. "They throw the ball and then fall down." Pretty concise description in my opinion. Sports was about socialization for me.

After we had met again at the Governor's Honors testing, Snell called my school and asked Frances if I was dating anyone. Honey, I was dating everyone. I was having the time of my life. I was not velcroed to a boyfriend. I had done that. I was not doing it again.

Snell got my phone number and called me at home. He asked me out, and we set a date for the following weekend, December 14. He showed up at my house and rang the front door bell. I still lived at home with my parents.

LIFE IS HARD SOFTEN IT WITH LAUGHTER

He got the honor of meeting my 6'4" daddy, complete with a .38 Smith & Wesson on his hip. Daddy hadn't changed from work and was still wearing his gun. He had retired from the city of Atlanta School Detectives Police Force and was currently working for DeKalb Juvenile Courts.

I never really thought it was odd that my daddy always had a gun on, but apparently some of the boys who came to the door were a little startled. Of course, we had a cat named Thomas that was five and half feet long from his head to the tip of his tail. Thomas hit the screen door at eye level when the boys came to call. Between Thomas and Daddy, it is a wonder I had many second dates. Good thing they didn't usually meet Mama right off the bat. She was the intimidating one of the family.

Snell and I had a delightful time. I don't remember what we talked about. It surely couldn't have been sports. If that had been the topic of our conversation, it would have been lagging before we finished the salad course.

When he brought me home, he hesitated at the door, and we talked a couple of minutes more. I did not spend time on the front porch with a boy, that's for sure. Mama started flashing the porch lights within ninety seconds of my arrival home. Making-out was not an option! Snell kissed me good night, and I opened the door and went in. I closed the door and waited until I saw his car lights come on. I thought, "I am going to marry that man. He just doesn't know it yet."

Snell and I dated exclusively for the next year. One day in the spring, I asked him if he wanted to marry me. He said he'd think about it. About three months after that, I asked him if he thought we should get married. "Maybe. We'll see. If you find a ring you like, we'll see."

We'll see? We had never looked at rings. Period. Not Never. Not Ever. Noooope.

One June evening, we had gone to the movies and were killing time at a department store that was having an estate jewelry sale. I love jewelry and adore old pieces

19

of Victorian and Art Deco. We were looking at the case, and there it was. An Italian gold band, inlayed with mother- of-pearl and small bands of diamonds. Not an expensive ring, but it was stunning. I loved the uniqueness of it, and I do favor gold and white together. And it fit. The next day Snell picked me up to meet Frances and her husband, Fred. When we got into the car, he said "Will you marry me?"

About dang time, I thought. But, I hugged him and demurely said, "Yes."

Fred, Frances, Snell, and I went to the store and bought that mother of pearl and gold ring. The store also had a beautiful solitaire, and Snell picked that out to go with the band. We were set. It was the end of June. It had taken me six months to get him to the engagement stage.

Then, he had to ask Mama and Daddy if he could marry me. Remember, I am now twenty-six, and he is thirty-seven. "Mr. and Mrs. Ratledge, I would like to marry Marlene. Would that be all right with you?"

Daddy response was, "If SHE wants to marry you, then it is okay with me."

Mama looked at Snell and said, "She can always come home if she wants to." Thank goodness, I did want to marry him. I never felt the need to come home. Mama and Daddy loved Snell better than me sometimes.

Snell and I decided to build a house and plan a wedding. It was mid-June, and we have just become engaged. Now, we are looking at house plans and building lots. We built a beautiful house and planned a great wedding all in less than six months. And didn't kill each other.

We've been together since 1975. We've had a moment or two, but where I burst into flames, Snell simmers a little, and then it is all over. We just have become the ideal love story.

Must have been destiny.

Been There Done That

My friend Charlotte Scott is a doula. Do you know what that is? I didn't. She isn't a mid-wife, but she helps pregnant women and their husbands prepare for the baby's birth through various educational classes and exercise programs. Her job is to make the birth easier for everyone.

One morning, I receive a message from her. Charlotte was at one of the hospitals helping in a delivery. This one was the fourth baby to be born in seven days. She loves it. She is so good at her job that she is widely requested. Right now, she has been at the hospital for ten hours with a woman in labor. I feel for all of them.

Labor is exactly the right name for what it is-- LABOR. It is hard work and painful, and it can last a long time. I know. We went into labor about 10:30 p.m. on a Sunday night, but did not go to the hospital until 2 a.m. James was born at 8:30 Wednesday morning. We had complications because dilation stopped. He decided that even though he was three weeks late he would just back up and hide for a little longer. James was trapped too far and for too long in the birth canal for a caesarian. He was delivered with forceps. Long story, made short, but still very real. James was deprived of oxygen and is mildly mentally handicapped.

21

I wish there had been a Charlotte there for us. She might have realized something was going wrong. I try not to blame the hospital staff. From the time we entered the hospital, twenty-one babies were born. Every nurse will tell you a full moon is when babies decide to enter the world. It was hectic. I know I saw three different doctors while we were there.

This story isn't turning out to be as funny as I had intended it to be. HMMM. I'd better work on that.

Our pediatrician's nurse was named Janet Looney, and she was expecting at the same time as I. Janet was admitted to the hospital about thirty minutes after me. I swear, she screamed three times and had her baby. Three times! Baby. I was told to get up and walk some more. During the ensuing days that I walked those halls, Janet came from her room, and we'd talk.

Babies were popping out all over the place. My roommate, Sherry Whigham, was admitted during the late hours of Tuesday night or the wee hours of Wednesday morning. Her son, Joey, arrived about six hours later. Janet had since been discharged with her bundle of joy. I was still walking the halls and panting my way by the nursey. I would count the babies. Mine wasn't one of them.

Trust me, I walked a million miles before I was told "it could be time." Someone came in and told me that I was to be prepped for a C-section. Well, good, I thought. I had the epidural, maybe two or three times, by then. The epidural was one of the things causing the labor to slow. No pain, no gain was what was happening because of it. At least, something was about to happen. Suddenly, the fetal monitor alerted everyone that James was trying to decide whether to come out or not. He is still slow to make decisions.

I had more people than I knew what to do with in my room. I thought I was being wheeled to surgery, but I realized we were in a delivery room. Everyone was talking. The doctor informed me she was going to deliver

James. I was feeling panicky. Snell was being shifted all around the room. What do I remember about that time? The first memory was of one of the nurses telling someone else that her husband had ran over and killed their cat that morning. Dear God. When I think of that day, I always remember her story.

The other thing I remember was that the doctor said, "Look at all that black hair." Then a huge shift of pressure, and I saw my baby for the first time. Snell cut the real umbilical cord. I still have an imaginary one attached to James at all times. I said, "He has eyebrows." What? Well, I don't have eyebrows. I had to have mine tattooed on as my retirement present to myself. Crazy thoughts.

We were wheeled into the hallway where the trash bags and the dirty laundry bags had been stacked. There were so many women in labor and babies coming that there was no room for us. It didn't seem to matter. All I could focus on was I had a baby in my arms. Snell was holding onto me, and I HAD A BABY.

Mama and Daddy were brought back into the hallway with us, and we all stared at this little black-haired beautiful boy. He still has the most beautiful blue-black hair you have ever seen. He also has an olive complexion. He actually favors my daddy. I am winter-white, and Snell has a fair complexion, too. James never looked like he belonged to us. Some people would ask if we had adopted him or if he were our grandson because we were old and fossilized when we had him.

He is still beautiful. Brilliant in some areas, slow in others, and compassionate to a fault.

I wasn't allowed to return to work for a number of months. When I did someone asked me when I was going to have another baby. Been there, done that, had Snell fixed so I didn't have to do it again.

Happy Birthday Daddy

Often this Brother would say "I am not a religious man."
But his deed told more than words
And his life revealed God's Plan.
When a Brother needed comfort
In time of sorrow or distress
This Brother was forever there,
To bring a bit of happiness.
Of his Creed, he did not talk
But quietly went his way,
Making religion one with life,
By living it each day.
A better man than Bob never lived. Some might have
equaled, but none was better.
                    Grace Evans Ratledge

I found this poem behind a picture of Daddy after Mama died. I don't know if she wrote the poem or if it was something she found. Either way, it does describe Daddy.

My father, James Edward Ratledge, would have been one-hundred years old November 21, 2016. After he died, Mama said he never left. She often commented he was still sitting in his recliner, waiting for her. I believed her.

Even now, I think Mama is sitting on my right shoulder, and Daddy is on the left one. Both are whispering in my ears.

LIFE IS HARD SOFTEN IT WITH LAUGHTER

I can still see them walking hand-in-hand. Daddy at his stature of 6'4" and Mama at her 5'5" in her prime. They almost always held hands as they walked. As Mama shrank, she held her arm bent even higher and Daddy leaned over a little more.

They met on a blind date at the old Atlanta Water Works while working at White Provision Company in 1943. The Atlanta Water Works was a favorite picnic place. Mama said he was the handsomest thing she had ever seen. Mama first saw him as he was approaching the picnic site she and her friends were setting up. He was tall, had beautiful blue-black hair, and a golden olive complexion. He was wearing a white suit with a black shirt and a black sling supporting his injured arm. She said he was too beautiful to forget. They married May 1, 1944. Daddy never forgave World War II for separating them. I have over 761 love letters he wrote during his four years of service.

During part of WWII, he escorted military prisoners. I have his secret identification that he used. Once it was learned that his father, Luther Edward Ratledge, had been a train engineer before becoming a police officer and Daddy could do medical task and train repair, he was reassigned. Daddy built the first hot water shower on the 7th Hospital train in Europe. After that, Daddy taught other train personnel how he had run the lines so their trains could also have hot showers.

One night, when he was so sick and on morphine, he was back on that train. I spent the entire night, rebuilding a train engine with him. He told me what tool he wanted, and I handed it to him. In his drugged imagination, all those machines in that room were part of the engine. We did a good job, too. By about 4:30 in the morning, he told me to "fire her up and let's get moving."

When the Allied troops captured Adolf Hitler's private train, it was damaged. Daddy and his medical train happened to be in the same location. One of the officers on Daddy's train suggested they ask Rat to look at the damage on Hitler's train. Rat could '*jury-rig*' anything. I don't know what was wrong with the train, but it couldn't be moved further into Allied territory because of the problem. Daddy went over and did whatever was needed to get it moving again. While Daddy was working on the problem, a team of U.S. and Allied personnel were cataloging every item in Hitler's train.

Daddy reported the repair had been completed to the officer in charge. The officer and his team were in Hitler's private dining car. The officer picked up a small cream pitcher from Hitler's table, handed it to Daddy, and thanked him for his help. The pitcher has the swastika emblem and is marked with an Allied catalog number. When Daddy returned home from the war and told Mama about the cream pitcher, she wrote a note about what Daddy had said and stuck it in it. He told her receiving the little pitcher meant, "We had won the war!" (This cream pitcher was featured on Antiques Roadshow January 2019.)

Daddy could do anything from electrical work to plumbing and wood-working. He was a perfectionist. He even did a little blacksmithing on the old forge at my grandparents' farm. Daddy and his mother flipped houses before it was a popular thing to do. Mama's family place didn't have electricity or running water. Daddy installed their first furnace, stove, running water, and bathroom.

You name it, he did it. He was the builder, and Mama was the painter and designer. He built his grandson an airplane swing with a six-foot wing span and working joystick, rocking horses, and any other thing he thought his namesake, James, could want. Daddy made a table that was James' height and the legs could be extended to grow with him. They did a lot of drawing and coloring on that table.

He made an entire kitchen set, stove, refrigerator, cupboards and even a sink with a turning faucet for the kindergarten class of H.O. Burgess Elementary School (1955). That set was still in use some fifteen plus years later. Our class had wooden animals to paint that he cut from scrap lumber, too. One of my classmates mentioned remembering them.

While he was capable of many things, he dedicated his life to public service as a peace officer. His radio call number 185, changed to 585, for the City of Atlanta Police Department/Atlanta Board of Education School Detectives. In 1947, Atlanta developed specialized detective units within the agency. In 1952, The Atlanta Board of Education and the Atlanta Police Department joined forces to create the Atlanta School Detective Unit. In 1953, Daddy and Julian Stephens were the second and third officers to join Sgt. J. D. Nash, the Commander of this team. The School Detective Unit was the forerunner of what we now call School Resource Officers.

Daddy held the record for the most cases solved for over fifteen years. I have all of his old reports. Someday, I am going to write that book I promised him. Unfortunately, I only have his papers to rely on and regret we never found time to create his book.

He and Mama taught me to be independent and self-reliant. I learned how to lay a wooden floor, to use most any kind of tool, paint a room, fire a gun, swim, defend myself, and drive like a police officer with a blinking light and siren. He made sure Mama and I were loved and well taken care of.

Rat accomplished all kinds of things and helped many people. He was known by many different identities through his life. Best of all, Daddy was mine. And I miss him. Mama used to say there will never be another one like Bob Ratledge. No, there won't. I bet Mama and Daddy are holding hands right now. Happy Birthday, Daddy.

The Other Woman in Your Life

Who is she? What is her name? I know you have one in your life. In this day and age, we all do.

Our friend or fiend is Miss Marple, so named because she takes information from her community and surroundings to guide you. You may know her better as a GPS. Miss Marple has a distinctive voice, and she doesn't speak Southern.

She only knows HUGH-stone and not HOUSE-tun Street. Loganville is LOG-und-ville. VI-enna is VE-inna. Now, you know as well as I do that her pronunciation is just not right.

I have wanted to rip her wires out more than once when she has taken me around the world to get to where I wanted to be. Why can't she just use streets AND expressways to get you there in the most efficient way?

A friend of ours has Plain Jane because her voice is so flat. Plain Jane's favorite saying is "Make a legal U-turn." It might be that our friend misses a lot of the turns. Regardless, riding with him and Plain Jane can cause one very quietly to lose one's mind.

I must tell you that Miss Marple has been called some other names when I have been alone in the car. On those days when I am running the latest, behind a traffic slow down, and I hit every red light, Miss Marple tries to take me to the moon and back. I might say to her in my calmest, most soothing voice "Oh, shoot, Miss Marple. There must be a better way. Dang it, even I know a way that is better than what you are taking me, dear Miss Marple." Well, I might not have said it quite like that.

You know, I think she can really understand. And I am sure she retaliates by creating new ways of getting to places. The more aggravated you become, the more turns and twists in your directions she makes. Really. Pay attention next time. When you put in fastest time, see if you don't end up in the worst traffic jam on the expressway. Tell her you want the shortest distance and I bet you go ten miles out of your way. There is never a most direct route.

If I take a different way than Miss Marple wants me to drive, she demands that I turn somewhere and then turn again and then turn again. She gets really aggravated and demanding. You know, now that I think of it, she does have something of a hateful voice.

I was coming home from the far side of Dacula (DACK-you-LAH). Miss Marple and I had a gentle conversation about how she just possibly had made a mistake. I knew enough to know that Snellville was not in the direction of Buford (BUFF-ford). When I saw the road sign indicating I was entering Carl, Georgia--CARL? I knew I was in trouble. Where in blue blazes is CARL, Georgia? All I knew was I was in Carl, and Miss Marple had me under her control. I knew of no way home, and that meant, she was in charge. I swear she snickered. By the way, Carl is the only name she pronounced correctly.

I pulled over on this wild goose chase and hit the home button again. She brought up a completely different map this time. Following her directions, I went down every pig path and side road. I had to do several legal and illegal U-turns. Eventually, I got home. The trip should have taken 30 to 45 minutes. Two and half hours. Snell was about to call the state patrol because, of course, my phone couldn't get a signal for 97 percent of the time on my journey to nowhere.

We recently stopped at the Georgia Welcome Center where I got a paper Georgia and an Atlanta paper map. I will learn how to refold them, and they will always be in the car. I may do no more than slap Miss Marple with the maps, but I will feel more comfortable with some old-fashioned technology that doesn't talk back.

What is in Your Christmas Stocking

Christmas presents. Oh, I hate shopping for Christmas presents. I have a very small family for whom to shop, but still I feel like I am never good at picking out the right gifts for them.

I guess we have reached the age where when we need something or want something, we just buy it. I know that is what Snell and I do. One year he bought himself a steering wheel for the 1948 Cadillac, and we called that his Christmas gift. I came home one day and told him that he didn't need to worry about getting me a present. I had bought my 40th anniversary and Christmas present. He said, "Do I like it? Did I do good?" I told him he had excellent taste, and he was thrilled that he had found something I loved so much. Are we pathetic, or what? No matter, we are happy with our arrangement.

Our son gets Christmas surprises. Well, they are rarely surprising. He either finds them wherever I have hidden them, or he just tells me what he wants. But one year, he was really and truly surprised. Actually, so were we.

Jimmy, Snell's brother, was better known as Jimmy Buck by most people and Ucca Buck to James. He and his wife, Debbie, managed Silverwood Farms, a ranch for people who boarded their horses. It also provided a wooded area and open fields for people to ride.   James loved to fish in the several ponds on the property with his Aunt Debbie. There are a lot of memories of that

31

ranch. Snell's buckskin cutting horse of twenty-three years, Sealy, lived there and is buried on the ranch.

It has been tradition for the three of us to gather every Christmas Eve with Snell's family for dinner and presents. We rotated Christmas Eves between our homes. I should have been suspicious when Debbie called and asked if we could do our holiday at their house this time. Well, sure, any time I didn't have to cook and clean the house was okay with me.

We had a lovely time, eating and laughing and opening presents. Our niece Emily had just turned two and was having the best time with the wrapping paper. James, who was seven, had gotten something with which he and his Maw-maw, Miss Bobbie, were enthralled.

Snell's mother was known as Miss Bobbie to many people. She taught first grade at the Snellville Consolidated School until her arthritis became so severe she could no longer work. Bobbie Snell Buchanan was one of the most loved people in Snellville.

We noticed that Debbie and Jimmy were gone. Before anyone could get up to find them, Debbie opened the back-door singing "Merry Christmas, James!"

Jimmy walked in the kitchen door leading Cricket, a Shetland pony. All the air left the room as we gasped in unison. James was so stunned that he could only look at Cricket. He really couldn't move. Finally, he slowly got up. He walked toward Jimmy, just staring at Cricket and Ucca Buck. Jimmy was laughing so hard he was in tears. Debbie, who was James' favorite person in the whole room, scooped up James and put him up onto Cricket's back.

From the time James began talking, he never stopped, but he stopped this time. He just looked from Cricket to Jimmy to Debbie. Then, he started to smile.

Home and Life

"I really don't mind cooking if you do it."

Coffee My Elixir of Life

I have had a lifelong love affair with coffee. I call it my elixir of life. My affair with this strong, vibrant, hot potion began at a young age. My granddaddy would pour a little of his coffee with a lot of milk into his saucer and let me sip from the saucer. He died just before I turned three. I only have a few memories of him, but those memories are vivid. His coffee in a saucer is one.

I remember being at Mama's family home in Eastman, Georgia, and drinking my bottle of coffee. I know now that it was milk with maybe a teaspoon of coffee added. Whoever fixed "the baby's coffee," fixed the milk with just enough coffee to give it flavor. The milk came warm from the cow, too.

My grandmama made STRONG coffee. We called it the Smith-Evans brew. Her elixir would cure what ailed you. Insomnia, you pass out from the fumes. Narcolepsy? Never again. Pin worms, tape worms, all dead by the time you stand up from the table. Thick blood, her coffee thinned it down. Thin blood, her coffee thickened it. Ticks and fleas couldn't live if they bit you and mosquitoes turned their little feet to the sky. They died from caffeine-induced hyperactivity. Grandmama's formula cured it all. My cousin described our grandmama's coffee as "One cup was strong enough to make most people able to thread a sewing machine needle while it was still running."

She had an old percolator that must have been 100 years old when I was little. My mama had one, too. Come to think of it, so did all of my aunts. They all "cooked" coffee the same way. The grounds were probably bleached white by the time it had finished perking.

After breakfast, Grandmama made another pot of coffee and put it on the side of the wood stove where it would stay warm all day. If you wanted a cup of perk-me-up, you set the pot back on one of the eyes of the always hot stove. In just a few minutes, you had hot, black, eat-the-enamel-off- your-teeth coffee. It was always ready, but it may have needed a little water to dissolve the syrup it had become. Good stuff!

My daddy loved strong coffee, too. His normal routine would be one or two cups in the morning, but there were exceptions. He would have another cup if Mama made breakfast for supper or if she made toast with her homemade fig preserves for a snack.

When I was child, I stayed at my Aunt Hazel's during the summers and school holidays. Hazel had a huge garden at the bottom of her long, steep driveway. In the back of the main house, she raised rabbits, chickens. and two sheep. The two sheep, Dolly and Molly, were there to help control the kudzu. I was glad when she got rid of them. They were mean and stank to high heaven.

Hazel and I would have our coffee with breakfast each morning before starting the day's chores. By this time, I was into the real stuff. One cup of coffee was worth two trips to the bathroom. Remember that. Hazel and I would get all our tools together and ride the tractor down the hill. Once there, we unloaded our tools and baskets for work. About noon, we'd get back on the tractor and head back to the house to make a coffee deposit. Of course, we drank another cup of coffee while we were at the house. That old tractor logged a lot of miles up and down the driveway.

The first time Snell had coffee at my parents' house, his eyes opened really wide, kind of popped out, and then rolled slowly back in his head. His front teeth started to chatter, and his hands shook. I think he emptied all of Mama's little milk jug into the cup. After that, he asked for only a half cup and filled the rest of it with milk. He swore Mama's coffee would send him to the Promised Land a lot faster than anything else in this world. Snell has begged me not to make the Evans-Smith-Ratledge coffee brew. I added the Ratledge name as my contribution to my grandmother's famous concoction.

I have had a couple of coffee makers through the years. When Snell and I married, we had an electric coffee pot. I used that pot for years. Snell's sister and her family recently gave us a Keurig, a gleaming white machine that makes coffee in just a minute. I hate to say this, but I think it was in self-defense. They have had coffee at my house before.

My old drip coffee maker continued to claim its space on our kitchen counter beside that fancy machine. Snell, James, and anyone who came to the house had a choice between fancy coffee and my turn-your-toes-up brew. I think Snell's cousin, Charles, was more thrilled with the Keurig machine than anyone. He said my coffee was so strong it dissolved his spoon and burned out his back teeth. He stopped saying that after he had a cup of Mama's. According to him, mine was weak as ninny water in comparison.

Truthfully, you just can't make really good coffee in a pot that isn't well seasoned with years of past grounds and a little aluminum flavoring. Hopefully one day I will find Mama's little percolator in one of the many boxes that have her belongings. It will be a joyous celebration for me. I wouldn't be at all surprised if Mama and Daddy didn't park their angel wings next to the kitchen door to have a cup of coffee with me that day. Unless my grandmama is "cooking" her coffee in Heaven, I'm positive they have not had a good cup of coffee in a long time.

Cooking is not My Forte

I don't know what got into me. I am no domestic goddess. I am a diva. My idea of cooking is making reservations, reading my favorite take-out menus, or having Snell drive us to one of our regular eating spots.

One morning, I got up and thought, "I would really like some of Mama's Irish Stew." First mistake— thinking. Second mistake— seeing that I had all the ingredients. Third mistake— seeing a gluten- free cookie mix.

I actually started cooking. You should mark this date on your calendar. It is Super Bowl Sunday. And, I am pretty sure Hell is freezing over.

On the rare occasion I find myself inspired to make Mama's Irish Stew, I usually use cubed sirloin for this soul-satisfying dish. But for some reason, this time I had three cans of Hereford's roast beef.

Mama always kept a few cans of Hereford's roast beef on the shelf in case of emergencies. She could make some amazing things like gravies or hash with it. Mostly, she kept it for our little dog Ching. As he aged and became more infirm, Mama heated the roast beef and feed Ching the gravy and pureed meat. OK, now you know. My stew story involves good quality dog food from our pantry.

I had an onion that wasn't too fuzzy, so I cut off all the suspicious parts and diced it up. (Don't you love it when you can use fancy words like diced?) My version of

38

dicing an onion entailed me standing over the pot, holding the onion far away from me, and cutting it. I hope you didn't expect me to stand at a cutting board with a sharp knife acting like one of those chefs on the Food Network. Finished with the task of my version of dicing an onion, I went to the kitchen sink to wash out my eyes and blow my nose. (Sounding more delectable with every description, isn't it?)

Potatoes and carrots were next. Do you eat your carrots as you go? I do. I washed them and let them drain while I cut up the potatoes. Each time I came back to the counter, I ate another carrot.

One very important component to Mama' Irish Stew was her secret ingredient— McCormick's Beef Stew Mix. The night that Snell and I moved into our first house, I was going to be so good and make this beef stew for us. I even lit a candle for a little romance. I did everything I was supposed to do, except that I didn't know about Mama's McCormick's Beef Stew Mix secret. I finally called home and had to admit that I had tried to cook the stew, and it was bland. My daddy, who was the most supportive person in the world, started to laugh. He told Mama my dilemma and she started to laugh. She asked what I had put into the stew. I told Daddy, who relayed the details to Mama. Her response to Daddy was to inquire, "Didn't you add the Beef Stew Mix?" Well, no. I didn't know she had held that secret from me. She informed Daddy, who informed me (I don't know why she didn't take the phone) that the stew I had made was edible. She suggested I add more salt and pepper to give it a little flavor. They laughed about my first dinner for the rest of their lives.

Pleased with the bubbling brown liquid infused with the canned roast beef, onions, potatoes, the few carrots that I didn't eat, and Mama's secret ingredient, I knew the best results for the stew was slow cooking. My stew was stewing, and I was still channeling my inner, repressed Paula Deen. I decided to mix up the gluten-

39

free chocolate chip cookie dough. As instructed on the back of the box, I pre-heated the oven.

You need to know that gluten-free is just a nice way of saying sweetened ground cardboard. As the oven heated, I parched pecans and mixed them in real butter with a little salt. I succeeded in making charcoal. Charcoal is good for you, isn't it?

As I proceeded to burn the pecans, I didn't notice the aroma of browning, uh, blackening, cookies. Most of them were okay. James broke them up and gave them to the birds outside, who seemed to like them.

We ate dinner. No one threw up or died. Super Bowl Sunday passed with no one going to the ER. I'd say I had a pretty successful day of cooking. I might try this again next Super Bowl. Don't hold your breath.

Home Cooked Meals

Y ou all know how I feel about cooking. I really don't mind cooking, if you do it. A kitchen was included in our house, but it was strictly for resale value. Someone, who I thought knew me better, told me she needed to replace her thirty-year-old cookware. She asked me what kind I had and if I was pleased with it. "Oh yes, I am very pleased. It is still almost new, and I have had it for over forty years now."

Then, she foolishly asked me what I had (I don't know) and if I had to replace it, would I get the same thing. I finally told her I had replaced all my cookware with neighborhood eateries and promptly gave her my list of local restaurants.

Recently, I ran into someone else at Kellie's in Loganville. She said, "I only see you here on Mondays."

My response to her was, "Monday is Kellie's for pork chops. Come on Friday, and I will see you again for Jimmy's unbelievable ribs." We have a place for every night of the week.

We do add a new place every now and then when we have found another restaurant family to adopt us. Yes, I consider the cooks and waitresses family. We go often enough that we know them all by name and know all about their families.

My mama cooked every day. She made a full breakfast and dinner. Daddy hated to eat out. Mama didn't like to cook and always said she was not a good cook. Mama was a superior cook as were her sisters. I asked her one time to make fried okra and fried chicken. She told me how to cook the okra and go buy the chicken from Colonel Chicken (KFC). She wasn't frying another chicken for the rest of her life.

Mama's sister, Sweetness, her real name was Hortense, was famous for her fifteen-layer cake made in an iron skillet. The chocolate sauce was to die for. Thick enough to be yummy, thin enough to ooze. Her son, Sonny, can make it, but I can't. I tried. I think you have to have her skillet and know how to hold your tongue just right. Sonny won't tell me, but I am sure there are secret words you have to mumble.

My Aunt Hazel made biscuits every day. I spent my summers and school holidays with her and Uncle Herman. Hazel was another mama to me. I would watch Hazel make biscuits. I have her recipes and her biscuit pan. I have made biscuits while she stood next to me. I do not make biscuits. I make little hard white stones. They are excellent for lining your flower beds. Nothing can or will eat them.

"Honey, I just don't understand it. I was standing right here telling you exactly what to do." Hazel would just shake her head and throw another pan of my rocks out the back door.

Another woman that I thought knew me pretty well asked, "Don't you ever cook? Don't you miss home cooked meals?" Geez, get over it. Snell said when he retired, he would take over the cooking. He did, and after three months, James and I fired him. You can only eat chicken with some sort of sauce on it so many times a week. At least when he did cook it was better than what I could do.

I was going to be the ultimate mama to our one and only child. I was going to cook fresh foods and puree them for James. I successfully made turkey dust. I took perfectly good green beans and made rope. My squash was shoe leather. Who can ruin boiled squash? Me, that's who.

Snell's mother, Miss Bobbie, was crippled with arthritis. She had to take early retirement from teaching because of it. She taught first grade for many years. Snell is eleven years older than his brother and fifteen years older than his sister. He did most of the cooking for the family. He said his daddy could fry an egg so hard you couldn't even use it for a rubber gasket.

I figure if you know every staff member in the restaurant and get invited to their weddings, baby showers and graduation ceremonies that makes you family. If it is family, then it is a home cooked meal at one of my family's houses—Kellies, Baby Jane's, Sam's on Main, Cup & Saucer, and Main Street. I am pretty sure Colonel Sanders was a cousin seven times removed on my daddy's mother's cousin's wife's side of the family.

The Sins Committed Against Red Eye Gravy

Jan Snell Houston sent a message about red eye gravy out on Facebook. Jan loves cooking shows, and she is an excellent Southern cook. I do not watch cooking shows because I am highly allergic to cooking. But I do love to eat. I know Southern cooking and Southern recipes.

RED EYE GRAVY has always been the cooking of country ham with coffee poured into the rendered fat. Recently, five well known chefs on the Food Network referred to flour-based gravy served over Country Fried Steak as red rye gravy!!! Most disturbing was one of the chefs was Trisha Yearwood. She's a Georgia girl and should know better. Along with Jan, I was appalled. They need to redo the show. That was just blasphemous! What do they pay researchers for??? Get a Southern cookbook, for heaven's sake. Trisha Yearwood hang your head in shame.

Red eye gravy gets its name from the 'red eye" created when you pour coffee in the warm meat renderings. The coffee pushes all of the fat away from the center and makes a red "eye" in the pan. This is a recipe that dates back hundreds of years. People didn't have a lot, and they didn't waste food. When you cooked your meat, you made gravy and then wiped out the cast iron pan with a biscuit or hunk of bread. A biscuit was a delicacy. To make the left-over pan juices go farther, coffee was poured in the grease, stirred and the gravy was poured over whatever you were eating.

Cured ham and bacon were meats that traveled more easily than other types. They were usually salted or smoked. The outside formed a crust to help preserve the cured meat. Where do you think Honey Baked Ham got the idea of slathering sugar on a ham? In the old days, sugar was dearer than salt. It was kept under lock and key in Sugar Safes.

Cowboys knew how to make red eye gravy. Do you really think the predecessors to John Wayne and Gene Autry carried milk, flour, and ground beef in their saddlebags to make "country friend steak" with flour based gravy, more commonly known as milk gravy? No, they had hard tack (strips of dried, salty meat), coffee, and water. Ground corn was often carried and sometimes dried apples or other dehydrated fruit. They didn't make filet mignon and fresh carrot salad on those lonely trips. The only fresh things on many of those trips were horse and cattle apples. Trust me; you don't want to eat those.

The amount of gravy one had was determined by the amount of fat rendering, how much coffee was on hand, and how much cooking time you had. My grandmama made it every time we "went home" to Eastman, Georgia. My daddy loved her cooking. My mama and her sisters, Hazel and Sweetness, made it. Their red eye gravies were never the same as their mama's.

How do you eat red eye gravy? I love it best on grits. Please, tell me you know how to make grits. Many people just pour it on meat or biscuits. My uncle poured it on everything.

Turn your nose up to red eye gravy, if you want. I promise you, if you ever eat the real thing, you will never want another kind. It tastes and is better for you than the pre-packaged gravies you find in the grocery store, and it doesn't have processed sugar and artificial flavorings. It is just good stuff poured over grits and eaten with pure joy. I wish I had some right now.

Wonder what Jan is doing for breakfast tomorrow morning? I bet she could go for a plate of salty ham, eggs, grits, red eye gravy, and coffee with real milk. YUMMMM

RIP Dear Coffee Pot

I am truly in mourning. My old coffee maker died. It bled out all over my counter, causing water to go everywhere. I took the pot off and dumped as much of the water out of it I could and then mopped up the rest. It was a sad, sad morning.

You all know that I begin my day with a pot of coffee, not a cup—a pot. It isn't a good day until I've had about 32 ounces of coffee kick-starting my brain. The day my brain dies, my heart with keep pumping the caffeine for seventy-two more hours. Cremation may be a problem with all the liquid inside. On the other hand, I may be pretty well preserved from it.

My friend and I have been together for more than ten years. I guess that was a lengthy life expectancy of a coffeemaker that probably provided two pots of coffee a day.

My sister-in-law and her family gave us a Keurig coffee machine. I think they did it in self-defense. My coffee is NOT ninny water and is designed to make you stand up straight and dissolve all your inner barnacles. I used the Keurig today. It made good coffee. It wasn't my level of strong coffee, but it was passable. I found that I needed twice as much to get my buzz on, though.

Now, the difficult part has started. I must seek out a new coffeemaker. I cannot find my mama's old percolator. If I could, that would be my choice of replacements for my dear friend. Mama's percolator made the best coffee, but somehow it is gone. I am accepting recommendations for coffeepots. If you have one that you think does the job with excellence, let me know.

I wish stores would let me come in and make a pot to sample. I would buy the one that proved to be the best in a heartbeat.

By the way, Snell told me I could not bury my dear old coffee maker in the cemetery with all of our animals and family members. I don't understand why not. I loved that pot more than many people I know.

Hoarder vs. Collector

I am the first to admit that I have collected a lot of things. Probably, I should get rid of most of them. I can't. They have someone's name on them. Almost all of my stuff is hand-me-downs, or something salvaged after someone's funeral.

I don't think of myself as a collector or a hoarder, more like a protector of things that once belonged to family. I don't know why I feel the need to salvage and protect what remains of my ancestors' belongings. My son, James, isn't interested in all this stuff, but me—I love it all. Our niece and Snell's sister do not care for my style of preservation. Snell is like, "I saw it. It's ok." He won't pay any attention to it ever again.

I love Victorian. The more curlicues it has and the harder it is to clean the more I love it. We have a house full of dust catchers. There is no denying it. It is all there for anyone to see.

My maiden name is Ratledge. My art students called me either Art Woman or Miss Rat. Over the years, I have managed to accumulate a number of mice figurines, mostly as gifts from my kids. Occasionally, I will see a mouse that must come home with me, but most of the critters came from my students and friends. Each one is special. Each one has a story associated with the giver. Most of my smaller sized pieces of the rather significant rat collection sits on my grandmama's sewing machine. Daddy rebuilt it, and it is a working treadmill Singer.

Then, there is the accidental collection of teapots. I found some old teapots at my grandmama's. My Aunt Hazel had one or two in her stuff. Mama had two or three in her stuff. Somehow, they all ended up in my stuff. They are displayed on top of the kitchen cabinets and the china cabinet. I didn't start out to collect teapots. Actually, I have never bought a teapot. People noticed that I had a couple, so they started giving me more. Now, they are part of my stuff, and I can't give them away.

My grandparents had an old wooden box stored in the crib on their farm. It was full of demitasse cups and saucers. I did manage to sell some of those, but many are now displayed in odd places around the house.

Oh, let's not overlook the rocks. Mama loved rocks. She and Daddy placed them around her flower beds. He made patios and walls with them for her. When we sold her house so that she could live with us, we brought the loose garden rocks here. Is that a collection?

Part of the sunroom furniture came from my Uncle Herman parents' house. Another part came from the old barn at my mama's family farm. I did have to wait until the resident wharf rat moved on to bring home the old buttermilk blue feed bin. The rat hole is perfect for running the wires from the computer and phone. I also have a great buttermilk-blue toolbox that makes a perfect coffee table. (A lot of bleach was used on everything!!!) Oh, there is the chest that held ammunition. It is perfect for storing printer paper.

James collects things, too. He started with china animals, especially birds and elephants. Then other animals came. Now, he is into all kinds of video games. He also blows glass and does photography. We have a vast collection of his artistic endeavors.

Our living room furniture belonged to Daddy's mother. Hard as a dang rock with itchy horsehair covered with ugly navy-blue fabric. Mama had it recovered. It was in their house until she moved, and then we got it. I had planned to recover it in white on white for my blue living room until Mama looked me in the eye "Why recover it? It has hardly been sat on. I had it redone in 1972." It was in perfect condition, although it was cream, orange, and green-striped fabric, and it was currently the year 2008. Mama was alive. The furniture looked brand new. I would have to keep it covered in sheets because of the cats. White on white with a dusting of cat hair wasn't very practical, and I didn't have the strength to fight Mama on this one. Mama is gone, and the cream, green, and orange furniture is still there, covered in sheets.

Some of our other furniture belonged to Snell's Aunt Kate. There are pieces that were his parents, who passed it on to his grandmama and Aunt Myrtle before coming to our home. It was done in industrial strength gold plastic upholstery. That stuff was indestructible. Ugly as homemade sin, but still perfect. I did redo it into a nice blue, purple, and gold floral pattern. Of course, I do have my Aunt Hazel's furniture, along with some of my mother-in-law's furniture. My uncle left me my great grandmother's bed. The 1965 stereo upstairs has the complete collection of Paul Revere and the Raiders albums. Classics, every one of them.

The dining room suite was Mama's. The dishes decorating the walls were my grandmama's. This past year we actually bought new den furniture. The last time we bought furniture was when we married, in 1975. Daddy told me he would give me money to use for either the wedding or for whatever we needed. It was our decision. I thought, "Let them eat cake," in the church basement. We proceeded to buy bedroom furniture, a kitchen table, a hutch, and a couch. Why put a ton of money into a wedding when you can have a semi-furnished house instead!

My biggest collection is cat hair, however. I get a fresh crop every day. The amount depends on the catitude around here. Are the cats a collection? James keeps finding strays to bring home. Does four in the house, three outside make a collection? OOOH, maybe.

Am I being a hoarder? I am still working on the definition of hoarders versus collectors. I do admit to being a sentimentalist. Definitely. Appreciative of old things? Yes, certainly. I just have memories of things that have brought us and our family pleasure over the years. That's it! I am not a hoarder. I am a **protector!**

I probably need to protect a little less stuff.

Dust is Just

D o you love housework? Are you thrilled to polish silver? Is scrubbing bathrooms the highlight of your day? Would you rather reline your kitchen shelves than eat chocolate? Would cooking a seven-course gourmet meal thrill you to death?

When I win the lottery, I want a chef, a housekeeper, and a chauffeur, in that order. But, until that happens, I have discovered a way to beat the drudgeries of housekeeping.

Dust is just. There is a reason why all of my furniture is covered in dust. I can justify most anything, but dust just makes good sense. No, it is not that I am lazy and hate to clean. Dust, however, is a protective barrier. It is much harder to scratch furniture when it is protected by a soft layer of dust. It acts as a preservative by sealing in all the natural oils and protecting the furniture from the harmful rays of sunlight.

Be kind to flora and fauna. Spiders have to have a place to live. I wouldn't want to spend my entire life living in a corner, but if the corners of rooms make them happy, leave them alone. The webs give a softness to the hard edges of a room. They diffuse light, so you have a softer glow in the room. They eat mosquitoes and bugs. PETA gives you brownie points for allowing them to live. I think it helps if you name them. Agatha Tarantula and Mavis the Merry Widow are very content with the status quo. I wouldn't consider disturbing their peace of mind.

53

I wonder if you can get an agricultural land tax deduction for spider farming.

Windows are the eyes to the world. I have a lot of windows because I wanted to let in the light and the beauty of the great outdoors. Dumb idea! Two parts white vinegar and one-part water makes an excellent glass cleaner. Wipe the glass with coffee filters for a lint free surface. Do you really want to smell vinegar and scrub windows? And what do you see when you look outside—grass that needs cutting. PUH-lease!

Refrigerators protect food from contamination. Okay, we all know about penicillin and moldy bread. We must continue to do research. Unless the green fuzzy thing on the back of the second shelf growls at you, the refrigerator is fine. Just name them all happy names. Fuzzy-Wuzzy, Peach Blossom, Strawberry Hazy, and good ol' Milky Way have been with us since I tried to learn to make bread.

Lustrous, beautiful silver? One of the worst wedding presents you can give someone. I tell people that I had mine dipped, so it will have that lovely blue-black color. Hey, if you shine that stuff you are removing some of the valuable silver, and it just oxidizes all over again. Isn't it better to keep the value by not cleaning? I mean Antiques Roadshow tells you to leave things in their original condition and not to refinish them.

Whoa! Better get that winning lottery ticket. Milky Way just tried to bite me.

Hissy Prissy

My computer's name is Hissy Prissy. She is prissy with her lavender colors. She knows how to throw a hissy fit, which she does regularly. She can be the most hateful thing in the world. What she does is set you up for success. You are working hard and doing well. She turns frigid on you without any warning or hint of wrong doing on your part. No lover can be more spiteful or fickle.

Even when I threaten her life support, Hissy will glare at me with her cyclop's eye and hum a dirge. She knows how to get my goat. I regularly threaten to turn off her life support. Sometimes, I jerk her life line from the wall. When she is resuscitated, she behaves for a time. I know she is using that respite to plan her next attack on me.

I have this wonderful computer guru named Lee Faile. We call him Buddy, and he has an understanding with Hissy Prissy. Cyber Buddy is his company's name. I just love it. He installed Team Viewer on my computer so when Hissy and I are in the throes of computer apoplexy, he can take over my system to fix everything without being in my office.

A lot of times he tells me to leave Hissy Prissy on and go somewhere else. I think I am much more of a hindrance than a help to him when he is working. He used to explain things to me on the phone while he worked. Now, I can just hear the smile in his voice as he says, "Miss Marlene, you just sit there and don't do anything." So, I sit there. I don't do anything. I think he decided all of my brain cells that were computer-oriented have been damaged in some way. He knows Hissy is smarter than I am.

One time, Hissy got hit by either a virus or lightening. I am not sure which, but she was sick. She lost consciousness, and nothing I did would revive her. Buddy said he would triage Hissy into his hospital to run a CAT scan (Computer Attitude Test), an MRI (Media Restricted Information), and other diagnostic evaluations.

We transferred guardianship of Hissy Prissy from me to him. Buddy called the next morning to tell me he was going to put in a new hard drive (heart transplant). The procedure would entail him doing a complete download of all her memories (transfusion) so that she would not awake in total amnesia. My beloved Windows 7 would be gone. I would forever be doomed to Windows 10. Hearing me start to hyperventilate over the phone, Buddy assures me that both Hissy and I would be fine.

Buddy understands I am computer illiterate and perhaps a little computer apprehensive. He is bilingual, speaking computerese as easily as he does plain folk talk. When he is on Team Viewer with me and explaining computer things, I almost understand. I take copious notes with pen and paper. Buddy can take Hissy through the throes of agony in surgery on her hard drive, and she will purr when he was finished.

Buddy was able to save her. Hissy may have more parts than the Bride of Frankenstein, but she is alive again. Yes, that is me standing in the front yard screaming "She lives!"

I am just so appreciative and amazed with Buddy and his miraculous saving of Hissy, but it means little to her. He saved her life and what few sanity cells I have left, but Hissy still doesn't appreciate any of that. She still acts ugly.

LIFE IS HARD SOFTEN IT WITH LAUGHTER

I think I know why Hissy Prissy gets on these hateful spells. Hissy has a crush on Buddy. When she is feeling a little flirtatious or, ummm, lonely, she pretends to have a medical episode requiring immediate aid. Buddy gets on Team Viewer, takes her to heaven and back, and she is happy again.

Our Entertainment Center

Honestly, I sat down at Hissy Prissy this morning to do some work on other things. I really did, but now I am sitting here in the sunroom watching a mama deer and her yearling wander across the yard.

They have been raiding our bird feeders every night. We have feeders outside of our bedroom and sunroom windows. We call the bedroom window the cats' entertainment center. I have a very old Eastlake recliner in the window. It is one of the earliest recliner designs invented. I scrounged it out of a Dempsey dumpster.

Snell and I were taking a class in upholstery at Central Gwinnett Community School, and the recliner was the piece we carried to class every week. The teacher had never seen one like it. I thought we did a pretty good job of recovering it. You never see the upholstery work we did on it, though. The chair stays covered all the time with a sheet because the cats think it is theirs.

Back to the deer. There was just something calming in watching the deer walk through the yard. They stop to nibble at the grass or watch for predators with their regal alert stance. Our yards are covered in those tall dandelions. You can tell what path the deer took by the green aisles created among the yellow flowers.

I ran to get Snell and James, so they could enjoy watching them, too. The deer were standing close to the sunroom, seemingly looking in the windows. I guess they got bored watching us watch them, so they ambled to the bird feeders in front of the livestock's entertainment window.

We cautiously and sort of silently made our way to the bedroom. I say "sort of silently" because if you know James, my own bull in a china shop, we don't do anything silently. He was so busy telling us to be quiet that he made a racket.

The two deer scouted around and started eating seed from the ground. Mystic was beside herself with joy dancing on the top of the recliner. Her tail was thumping, and she was just mesmerized by the deer. I don't know what she would have done if she had caught one, but she was intently enjoying herself.

Gracie was standing on the floor with her front paws resting on the window sill. She doesn't meow like a normal cat. She "muffs," making her very long white whiskers tremble and cup forward. She also makes little "mik-mik" sounds. Gracie was just a-talking. Mystic was thumping, and James was busy telling us to be quiet. I don't know why, but the deer didn't run off. Maybe, we were more entertaining to them than they were to us.

Mystic's tom-tom beat and Gracie's "mik-mik" alerted Figaro that was something was happening. She did not want to miss anything. Figaro is a big cat, and she moves two ways—stalking and gliding. She glided into the bedroom and over to the window. "Move over, kiddos. Big Mama wants to see what's going on." Gracie was so fascinated she didn't move so Figaro could have the window. Figaro sat on her haunches and placed her front paws on the window glass.

There we all were. Three adults and three cats watching two deer gobble up five pounds of bird seed. We were all locked in for as long those deer wished to stay. You would have thought we had never seen a deer before. It appeared they were looking at us almost as intently as were staring at them.

"Hey, Ma. See the morons in the window?"

"Now, darling, don't talk ugly about the humans and their masters, those cats. They mean well, and they put out all of these good seeds and salt licks for us. Now, tip that feeder and let's have lunch."

One deer gently nudged the bird feeder so that the seeds would begin trickling out of the holes. The other deer leaned down, opened its mouth, and let the seeds slide right in and down its gullet. Then they switched places. We watched them empty the feeders. When all the food was gone, they gracefully turned, looked back over their shoulders, and walked away. Mama deer turned back one more time and twitched her tail as if to say, "Fill 'em up again, folks. We'll be back for supper."

Best Dust Catcher Ever

First, you need to know that I am a sentimentalist. A big one. I cherish old stuff that someone else touched. Most of our furniture and 98% of my dust catchers once belonged to someone in my family or Snell's. My father-in-law was not a sentimental saver, and neither is Snell's sister. They just don't have the deep need to keep things like I do. Snell's mama, Miss Bobby Snell Buchanan, was a protector of old things. Because Miss Bobbie and I were kindred spirits, I salvaged and brought home things she had managed to tuck away. Mr. William didn't care for dust catchers and clutter.

Mama and Daddy kept old things because they were good, long lasting quality items, and if they had belonged to a favorite person, so much the better. The furniture in the living room belonged to my daddy's mother. Hard as a rock, but it belonged to her.

We also have the living room furniture from Snell's family, too. First, it belonged to his Aunt Kate DeLoach (Mr. William's sister) and then to his parents. When Snell's parents decided to replace it, they gave it to his grandmother and his Aunt Myrtle. That three-piece suite lived on with Uncle Cyril Snell until it finally came back to us. It was originally upholstered in some dark-navy colored material and then industrial strength gold plastic. We recovered it in a pretty floral. It is of the same period as my grandmother's set, which means it also is hard as a rock. But it belonged to family.

There are things all over this house that I touch (note, I didn't say dust) that evoke a memory. An old vase that has lost almost all of the poppy picture that was painted on it belonged to my mama's maternal great-grandmother. It is a small thing, not worth the space it takes, but it will live here as long as I do. The house has more of just the same sort of useless treasures that once belonged to someone else.

Our son, James, blows glass. He has made some amazing things. We have his glass all over the house. Glass makes for fabulous dust catching. Our Christmas tree is a wrought iron sculptured tree covered with his blown ornaments of globes, birds, and turtles. A dear friend of ours collects James' orange pumpkins. Someone else wants his elephants, and I want it all, just because he made it.

From the look of this room I am sitting in, we also collect cats. All four are in here, shedding, making tumble-fur weeds. I try to explain to people that the tumbling fur weeds makes great protection for all the dust catchers. They look at me like I am crazy, probably thinking I need to clean my house. People just don't understand.

All of this brings me to my best dust catcher ever. We went to Snellville Harvest Festival this past fall. James wandered over to look at something in a booth that belonged to the Sunflower Bears ladies, Donna and Ginger. Their slogan was "Making Your Memories Huggable." They had all kinds of teddy bears made from various bits and pieces of old clothing.

In an old chest upstairs is one of my grandmama's dresses, printed with clusters of purple violets. There is also a pair of my granddaddy's overalls. My grandparents were farmers in Dodge County, Georgia. I found the clothes in an old trunk in the big barn at "Home," what we called their farm. Yes, I dragged the old trunk home, along with a couple of toolboxes and many other worthless items. I washed anything that was fabric and lovingly returned them back to the trunk with some other dust catchers.

In that trunk was a baby outfit that my granddaddy wore, an old seashell, my grandmama's purse, and her white dress shoes. Her hose were rolled and placed inside the shoes just like the day she left them. It was just stuff.

I talked to Donna of the Sunflower Bears about these fragile old items. She agreed to work her magic with some these pieces of fabric and make them into a bear.

I learned about the history behind Sunflower Bears while visiting with Donna and admiring her creations. Her daughter, Ginger, is a three-time cancer survivor and had two daughters. Her daughter, Ariel, died at four-half months to SIDS in 1994. Ginger lost her second daughter, Sarah, in December 2016, at the age of twenty-four to a shooting range accident.

Sarah's friends asked for various pieces of her clothing to remember her. Donna was concerned that if she did give Sarah's things to the friends, the items would eventually end up going to Goodwill. That was when the idea of making Teddy Bears from Sarah's shirts as gifts came to Donna. She thought how great it would be to help others who had lost someone dear. She could make those loved one's belongings huggable. One of Sarah's favorite quotes was, "I want to be like a sunflower so even in my darkest hour I will stand tall and find the light".

Sunflower Bears was born!

I washed, ironed, and packed my grandparent's items into an envelope. They were on their way to Donna to become a huggable teddy bear. My bear arrived yesterday. It was beautiful. Grandmama's old dress was the shirt and head. Donna was able to maintain the lace Grandmama had tatted on the collar as well as the smocking she had designed on the shoulders of her dress. The ladies had cut my granddaddy's overalls in a way to keep one of the pockets and the label. The red suspenders were there along with a darned hole in the foot. Delighted was an understatement for how I felt about the bear.

On my bear's fanny is embroidered the following:
"These are the clothes we used to wear. Hug it tight & know we are there."
Love, Grandmama Louise Smith Evans
6/4/1889-6/15/1967 &
Granddaddy Eli Evans 10/19/1889-
3/21/1952"

I don't know what will happen with all my treasures after I am gone. While I am still on this planet, they will stay with me, and I will love each of them, remembering those people who touched my memories from so long ago.

If you would like to contact Donna about making a bear for you, her information is below.
Donna Hansborough
Sunflower Bears
www.SUNFLOWERBEARS.com

Diagnosis: Techno Apprehensive

I admit to being technologically challenged. I miss my working days when I could call for tech support and a ninth grader would come to my office. The thirteen-year-old fixed everything for me. Smiling politely, he said, "It's all done, Mrs. B." More than likely the kid was walking down the hall telling his friends that he had just had to help another old geezer with a computer.

It was suggested to me that I should have more connections through social media to promote my book of essays. I have a Facebook page that gets looked at about twice a week, but it isn't dedicated to my book. I signed up for LinkedIn which proceeded to highjack my entire address book. I am still apologizing for that one.

I was told specifically to have a website and a blog. Okay, if I really have to, I will have a webpage and a blog. Apparently, it was not in the cards for me to do so. In the world of cyber, people like me are fresh fodder for the brotherhood of demons that feed off the techno-apprehensive.

After three days talking nicely with Go Daddy representatives who supposedly set up a web site/domain/blog in my name, I was confused. Did you know that you have to pay one group to have a domain name and another one to have a website? I'm not sure what else I paid for, a lot of frustration and aggravation, for one thing. Everyone promised me that this technical mumbo jumbo was easy, and ANYONE could do it. Go

Daddy and Word Press assured me that even though my skills were limited to a rather basic level, ANYONE could do this.

I was advised to use WIX, but to register my domain at Go Daddy. Somehow, I ended up with everything on Go Daddy and Word Press. I thought my domain was over here in the Snellville-Loganville area. Well, according to Go Daddy, it was not.

The helpful man at Go Daddy set up www.marleneratledgebuchanan.com as my domain. Two things were apparent here. One was that I have a long damn name. The Go Daddy representative told me to use the name I write under: Marlene Ratledge Buchanan. Even I can't spell it correctly half the time.

The second thing was my domain name exists only at Go Daddy. I paid for it to have a home where my friends, family, and those people I can coerce can find it, but it ain't there. Go Daddy said it's there. No, it ain't there. Nope, nowhere, no how, no matter how much I beg, pled and cry. Na-da.

Now, I am a really nice person. I try to do good things for people even when they don't want me to. I do not hurt animals or little children, well, perhaps a small exception for spiders. I have been known to weep openly over dead critters on the side of the road. I am nice to even the most undeserving people. I try to get away as fast as I can, but I am nice while trying to escape.

Why do Go Daddy and Word Press hate me? They said ANYONE can set up a website and a blog. Well, I do know that I am NOT just anyone, but still. You know the joke about your computer having the ID-10-T virus? Well, I didn't think I was quite that much of a computer idiot, but Go Daddy proved me wrong.

I have talked to people at both Go Daddy and Word Press, which are interconnected but will not talk to each another. One man was very nice. Of course, he was. He told me we were all set with a domain name and website, and I gave him my credit card number. Then, I told the world that I had an account and to contact me. Know what you get when you give a prostitute $153.63. Yep. That is exactly how I feel.

On Day Five of attempting to have a website/blog and not have a nervous breakdown, I had succeeded only in having screaming meanie fits that scared the cats. Go Daddy and Word Press were still telling me I had this stuff, and ANYONE could set it up. One woman fell just short of telling me I was an imbecile. Then, she kindly told me to give her between $800 and $1200 and she would set it all up for me. But ANYONE is supposed to be able to do all of this techno stuff. It was so simple.

Day Six morning started with Snell telling me I spend too much time on the computer and to stop using it, blah-blah-blah "You just throw a fit at it, it doesn't do any good, and you scare the cats." Then I grit my teeth and cuss at both Snell and the computer under my breath. My brain has begun to boil and ooze from my ears.

I swear I was going to beat this thing yet or die trying. You can contact Tom M. Wages Funeral Services for the details. They will probably have me by the day after tomorrow. I hope they're able to pry the keyboard from my hands and remove the grimace from my face.

I spent the day very calmly and carefully following the directions. I called the account people to explain that I couldn't find my domain name on the Internet. I told them that I couldn't access anything beyond the set-up pages on Word Press.

I diligently wrote down with pen and paper all the directions given by the representative. I followed those directions several times. When I called Word Press again and asked for help in finding my webpage I was told once more that help was available only if I paid more money. Interesting that the information given during the set-up was different now they have my credit card number.

A couple of days ago, a man named Tim from Word Press called and asked how I was doing with my new account. I explained that things weren't going very well at all. We discussed my issues with these accounts and how I had followed all the directions, outlining the end result. Finally, he admitted that my set-up did not provide me with the easy access to the account. The instructions that I had so carefully recorded and followed from the people who were "helping" me were not taking me to my domain. Those instructions only led me back to the place where the setup of the account began. I was going in a circle.

I had to come out of all other accounts and go into Google. Once there, I had to log-in, proceed to Word Press and then into the domain. That probably would have saved me a half a head of hair. Now, erroneously I think progress was being made.

I spent yesterday setting-up my blog, once more. There was my picture. That had been there before, OK. The font, the colors, the domain name and email name were all in place, again. I was all set. I was happy. ANYONE could do this. I was going to be fine. Tomorrow would be my first blog thingy.

Day Seven. I typed in my domain name on the search bar on my AOL page. Not there. My name came up with references to other things, but not my webpage. I went through the whole process that I had written down, back in through Google to Word Press. All the stuff I did yesterday, not there. Nope. I ate three Hershey bars and prayed I would not have a stroke.

The guy who has been calling me every other day offering to help me set up my Go Daddy and Word Press domains, security, blog and email address for $800 to $1200 or $50 for thirty minutes called today. I canceled the whole thing. What a glorious feeling.

Decluttering Your Home in 10 Easy Steps

Recently, I was reading in the on-line Southern Living (January 2018) magazine an article on decluttering your home with tips on how to give life to your inner neat freak. Laurey W. Glenn was the author. I was sure she is a delightful person. She probably lived in a scrupulously clean and well-organized home. Ms. Glenn said you could declutter your home and life in ten easy steps.

My left hind foot. I wanted to see proof that she did all that she said to do. I am, or at least before I retired, a very well-organized person. When I left at night my desk at work was clean except for a calendar, two baskets, and a lamp. My computer desk at home is a 19th century farm table from my grandparents that I salvaged from the barn. I have two two-drawer filing cabinets and a small table my daddy made for James when he was little. Straightening up my computer work area is at the top of every to-do list I make. Sigh. I really need to read and pay attention to Ms. Glenn. Let's see what she said and what I thought.

The article explained that everyone had a hectic life and demanding job. People just don't have time to "organize on the go," but Ms. Glenn explained if you follow these ten simple steps, your life will change for the better—forever. I interpret this statement as meaning that my coffin will be clear of clutter and dust. I thought the only way I can declutter my life is in death. But I had an open mind or a closed coffin lid, one or the other.

The article went one to say that many folks think a clean and orderly house was the result of a weekly cleaning crew and a personal organizer. It suggested you design a smart way of cleaning and adopt these ten, simple "keep tidy tricks". I was not sure I could afford a personal organizer to come into this house and stay long enough to get things orderly. If I had someone, I wonder how long it would be before that person started ranting at me that I was doing everything the wrong way.

Then there are Snell and James. They believe laying something down where they "can find it when they need it" (in six months) was the way to be organized. They have accused me of hiding their things because I put them in drawers. Is this the way it is in your house? THEY can't find something, and it is YOUR fault?

And the four cats. If I can't get them to police their tumble fur weeds, how was Ms. Glenn going to do it? Oh, for heaven's sake. Suddenly, I realize Ms. Glenn didn't have a place for potty boxes and feeding stations anywhere in this article. Ah Ha. She didn't have animals or kids or a husband. It was only she, and she had severe neat freak OCD (Overly Clean Domain).

Well, here were those ten "Keep It Tidy Tricks." I have paraphrased her article so that it isn't as long and so that I didn't plagiarize. First, I suggest you get a box of Kleenex. You will need it when you realize that you have lived your entire life in disorder and filth OR because you are laughing so hard at the OCD individual who lives alone and doesn't even have a pet telling you how to tidy your life. If your house is this organized, I want to come over and look around.

1. Keep clothes off the floor.

In the picture was an attractive laundry basket about half the size a two-drawer file cabinet and one-third the size the baskets I have in the two bathrooms we use. I do laundry almost every day, and there are only three of us. Granted, James wears a uniform, and he changes clothes as soon as he gets home, so he does wear two outfits a day, but the second one is usually clean unless he spills something on his shirt.

Ms. Glenn told us that having such a hamper would make those people who typically step out of their clothes and never pick anything up want to place their dirty garments in the attractive container. Oh yes, this hamper of natural material woven in a nubby texture will surely make the sloth in your family change his ways. The hamper in the example may hold one shirt, one set of underwear, a pair of socks, and maybe one leg of a pair of jeans. The other leg will have to hang outside because there isn't enough room for it in the lovely and stylish hamper. Don't even go there with damp towels. The natural fiber hamper will suck up all the moisture and discolor itself and all items inside. The author of the article didn't think about this laundry quandary. She probably washed all her dainties in the sink each night. My dainties are a square yard of material. Her unmentionables are probably two strings and a triangle of imagination.

2. Keep Beds Made and Nightstands Clear.

The author actually used this sentence: "The secret to a neat home (and a future good night's sleep) was a freshly made bed and an organized nightstand." Our son falls out of bed, stumbles to the bathroom, and falls in the shower. If he stopped to make up his bed, he would be at least twenty minutes late for work, and he would wake up the cat. The cat is not a morning person, either.

3. Make Your Mudroom Multitask.

I had to quote Ms. Glenn about her description of this area. "Designed to stand up to dirty shoes, this mudroom is a go-to place for dropping bags, boxes, and coats during the rush of a busy day. In a high-traffic area, it's important not only to spruce up the look, but also to make it less prone to disarray. Baskets store out-of-season accessories, such as winter accessories in the summer and swimming supplies in the winter, while a long bench creates an easy spot for taking off and putting on shoes (reminding adults and kids alike to discard muddy shoes near the door). Well-placed hooks keep coats and backpacks off the floor."

Really? I mean, really? How many shelves and baskets were we talking about in reality? This picture showed three baskets and perfectly lined up shoes. Oh, and don't forget the live plant in the room!

Do you place all your summer swimming supplies in a basket in your mud room for storage during the winter? Do you have only one coat per person to hang up? My boys and I are pretty well trained. Shoes go into the closet. The coats, if dry, are hung in the closet. If damp, they are hung in the laundry room (her mud room) to dry. But somehow, I just can't see me or them fitting into this room with its three baskets and hanging hooks. And where do you put the trash can and the kitty litter boxes? I also have a problem with someone who only has three pair of shoes. Another rant, another time.

4.   Limit Your Laundry.

I do like the idea of having a washer and dryer that can be hidden behind louvered doors. I really do. You and I know the doors are only closed if someone is coming over and the tops of the machines are covered with stashed items that don't have a designated place. I just loved these next ideas. Organizing things with open shelving and hanging space will give you a clear view of what needs to be done. Yep, seventeen shirts need ironing. Ms. Glenn suggests that we put our laundry supplies in pretty glass jars. This way you will always know when you're running low. Have you ever tried to pour a twenty-pound box of Tide into a pretty glass jar? Nuff said.

And, of course, don't we all have a colorful little pail to use as a handy catchall for dryer sheets and wayward socks? Everyone should have handy hanging space above the machines. I am 5 feet 3 inches tall, on tip-toes. Where do I keep the foot stool so I can reach the hanging rod?

And she advocated a front-loading washer. I had one. I fought mold and mildew daily with that thing. Drying it out, treating it with anti-mold products and still I couldn't win. I will NEVER have a front loader again. I don't care what promises are made.

5. Make your Entryway More Efficient.

Ms. Glenn stated that the front entryway was crucial to an organized home—it's a go-to spot where guests and family members corral hats, umbrellas, keys, and important mail. I thought that was my laundry/mud room. She suggested creating a formal entry way if you didn't have one. Placing a small table with a hand-carved wooden box to hold car and house keys, a table lamp, and a bamboo tray to serve as a catchall near the door was a perfect way to do this trick. She also suggested adding other pieces to this "small created entry way" like a hat rack.

My small created entry way is where we block the cats from escaping to the outside world. I can see myself wearing the bamboo tray as I lay prone over the small elegant table while the hat rack is twisted between my legs. The cat will be sitting on my back looking at me like the fool I am. What is your small created entry way like?

6. Create a Command Center:

"To tame clutter and tackle your family's endless to-do lists, consider incorporating a command center—including a work space, a spot for notes, and organized storage—along a previously unused space, such as a long empty wall, an awkward kitchen corner, or a hallway nook." Ms. Glenn's example included a built-in desk with storage or using a freestanding desk and cabinet combo to achieve the same results. Magnetic chalkboard paint above the desk provided a spot for notes, grocery lists, and weeknight recipe ideas. I had to wonder how large Ms. Glenn's house was to have all this unused space.

All right, y'all, is this happening at your house? Have you got an unused space that can hold a desk-cabinet combo and chalkboard? Her command post is my refrigerator door. It has a calendar and a little cup with a pad and pencil. It is also covered in pictures, a grocery list, and crap. I do throw things away from it regularly, sort of.

7. Keep Linen Storage Tidy.

She described her typical linen storage area as a place that could hold a lot more stuff than mine does. She refered to it as "the soft and fluffy version of a junk drawer." I loved that expression. Again, somewhere in this vast house, in which this author lives, must be an armoire, cabinet or a closet with tall shelves that make putting laundry away a breeze. The tall open shelves provided a place to keep bedding in plain view. She suggested that the cabinet have a designated shelf for each room. That way the neat freaks in your family can grab their own linens. How many sets of sheets do you have? I have two sets of sheets for each of the beds we use. One on, one off. The guest beds need only one set. I wash and put them back on the same bed.

This idea I do like. She suggested using all white bath and hand towels. I agree with that. Easy to wash, bleach and stack. My son has his own beach size towels, which are in his bathroom cabinet as are our towels are in our bathroom. I really don't want to see anyone walking around wet, naked, and needing a towel, do you?

She did give a neat tip about folding fitted sheets? She suggested that you wrap the fitted sheet inside of the flat sheet for "crisp, finished stacks." Really! I do fold my sheets, wrap one pillowcase around that bundle and stuff it all into the other pillow case. Everything for that one bed is contained. It is mostly neat, depending on your definition of the word "neat."

8. Declutter Your Closet.

I like a lot of what Ms. Glenn has to recommend for closet organization. She suggested we make our closets work harder at the job they have to do. She recommended finding another space to hang items that you don't wear regularly, like formal wear and coats. Yes, great idea. I couldn't agree more. We even do this. We have a closet for coats that is separate from all the others. It really does help and is in our laundry room. Snell and James' shoes go in that closet, too. I have an antique cupboard that was made on my great grandparents' farm. It is in my laundry room and holds all of one season's shoes. (I am a shoe lover.)

Ms. Glenn tip was installing shelves in the bottom half of a closet to hold shoes and handbags. You hang tops above the shelves. She said this method will put your clothing where you can see them better, and you won't tend to lose them. I have a problem with this one. For one thing, I am short. I can't reach the things on the top shelves without a step stool that I have to store somewhere. And by the way, who only has seven shirts and five pairs of shoes? Where are the pants and dresses? This lady must wear only black and have one outfit for each day. One pair of black heels, one pair of black flats, one pair of black sandals, and one pair of tennis shoes, probably black. Have you noticed that all the closets shown in magazines display very small wardrobes? I don't know about you, but I have a lot more clothes than all these people.

Every year, she suggested that you purge your closets of clothes, shoes, and so forth. that you haven't worn or don't fit. This one I can buy into. I do clean the closets twice a year as I change out warm and cool weather garments. I do the same with shoes. I store my out of season shoes in plastic tubs with the moisture wicking packets that come in vitamin bottles and new shoe boxes.

9. Utilize Every Inch.

Kitchens are probably the most used room in the house. Well, except for mine. Space can be a rare commodity. She recommended placing little used items, such as cake plates, vases, and large platters, in the upper cabinet spaces for storage. Makes good sense to me. I don't cook unless I really have to, so those items are stored for years before I see them. She suggested we keep the essentials in the lower cabinet spaces where they are easy to reach. Ms. Glenn did suggest cleaning out your kitchen cabinets at least once a year to remove worn-out, broken, or no longer used items, either giving them away or storing them elsewhere for future use. Who places a broken or worn out item back in the cabinet so it can be purged at the end of the year? Personally, if it is worn out or broken, I get rid of it when I find it. I don't put it back in the cabinets for purging later.

10. Tame the Tech.

Entertainment areas and related items are like coat hangers--turn off the light and they begin to multiply. How many remote controls are really needed? All those wires, boxes, and "just stuff" that accumulates around them will take over a room. Ms. Glenn arranged all this mess "in an intentional and stylish way". She suggested that you paint the inside of the entertainment cabinet a soft color in a flat finish. Then mount the TV at eye-level and push all the wires and cords through a hole behind the TV. We solved this problem with a flat screen mounted on the wall.

She suggested decorating the shelves with pretty, colorful items, such as books, and to use baskets or boxes to hold remote controls. Have any of you women ever had a man put a remote control in a decorative box and close the lid? Me, neither. Mine complain that the box is in the way and just adds more clutter.

I would like to refer you to a little essay I wrote some time back, "Dust is Just." Dust is an excellent protective cover for your furniture and other things. Letting your silver oxidize produces a lovely blue-black finish, thereby assuring your guests that you have fine antiques (and no butler). Tumble fur weeds and dust bunnies are amazingly helpful for rolling across the floor and gathering up other loose particles of dust and fuzz. They tend to hide themselves under furniture, only coming out when you have visitors.

I am sure there are people in this world who can and do live like Ms. Glenn suggests. I, personally, have never met one. I am not sure I would be able to trust him or her if we did meet. I would want to open up all their closets and drawers and see what was jammed inside. I just don't know how to live in a clutter free and organized environment, do you? If you do, please come to my house and help me.

Marlene's 10 Tips for Keeping Life a Little More Manageable and Livable.

1. Collect unused stuff.

Place a box somewhere to collect useable items that you don't need or want. I keep one in the garage. When I run into something that falls into this category, I just put it into the box. We do the same thing with clothing. I fold them up and place them in the box. When James was a baby, he outgrew his clothes every fifteen minutes, so I had a box in his closet. When he could no longer wear something, it went directly into that box. Every so often, I drop the box(es) off at a collection center or set it out if the American Kidney Foundation happened to be coming by collecting donations.

2. Be a Money saver.

Want to save money? When James no longer needed diapers, I took money dedicated for them and put it into a savings account. We were paid once a month, so I just put the amount of money for diaper service and disposable diapers into James' little savings account. We have a special needs trust for him that we kick started with this diaper money. Since that money was already designated during his infancy, we have never missed it.

3. Organize with a calendar.

Put a big calendar on the refrigerator and write down ALL appointments for everyone. At one time, when I was caring for Mama, Daddy, and lots of other people besides Snell, James, and me, I used colored pens to indicate who, what, where, and when for my own sense of order. I don't have to do that anymore, but it did save some brain cells while life was so complicated. ·

4. Do it NOW!

Deal with things, tasks, or anything when it comes up. I have a friend who will put off things that she feels will be hard or unpleasant. I learned a long time ago to get the hardest, longest, and/or most demanding job out of the way. I don't have the extra time or brain cells to fret over something. I just get it done and free my mind of that clutter.

5. Cheap time savers.

Save those moisture absorbing packets from vitamin bottles and shoe boxes. Place one or more packets where you store your jewelry or out of season items. Put a packet in a plastic bag with your cleaned silver jewelry. You will rarely have to polish anything again. You can also use a piece of cotton fabric with a spoonful of non-clumping clay kitty litter in it. Tie it with string, not a rubber band. Use it inside winter boots and shoes and clothing storage. It helps remove moisture and that stale odor.

6. Use hidden space.

I use plastic bins hidden under the beds. I have lots of items stored under beds, like out of season clothes, shoes, and other stuff that need to be protected. Toss in either the moisture wicking packets or kitty litter bags.

Be careful though. The contents of those little moisture wicking packets are poisonous, and you don't want kids or pets to get them. For paper items, I use the kitty litter. ·

7. Declutter and help others

Have a box for books and magazines that you don't want to keep. The nursing homes and hospitals in our area love to get these items. Books for Heroes which sends material to deployed troops and VA hospitals is always in need. (www.booksforheroes.org)

8. Organize by color and use

Organize closets by color and like items. All pants are together, separated by colors. Do the same with tops. Tops that are multicolor, choose the dominate color for placement. When you rehang a garment turn the hanger wrong (open) side facing out. At the end of the season you can see which items you don't wear and perhaps you will want to donate or consign them. ·

9. Quick fixes

Keep a bag of non-clumping kitty litter around and throw a handful onto any oil drips in the garage or any kinds of spills you want to soak up and sweep away. It is good on icy spots, too. It is just clay, so it won't hurt anything like salt can. I have a friend who puts a couple teaspoons in her potting soil to help with maintaining moisture levels in her house plants. ·

10.Be realistic.

Pets, kids, and people do leave a trail of belongings. Try to train them early in life or in marriage and do the best you can. This is not worth having a stroke over. When you can't stand the clutter anymore, eat two Hershey bars. Chocolate always makes life look better.

Turn on the Heat

Our friends, Coach John and Margie Sawyer, have this ongoing battle over the thermostat that has lasted for 55 years or more. Margie grew up in Mount Rainer, Washington. You know, where it is cold, wet, and they grow cherries. John is from Hawkinsville. That is South Georgia. Their blood types do not match. Margie rarely gets cold, and John rarely gets warm. Margie's rule is that you turn on the furnace on November 1, and only if it is absolutely necessary.

John's rule is when Margie is out of town on a business trip, he turns the heat on whenever he wants and as high as he wants. When she is due in, he turns it off. I think he finally just stopped turning off the heat. When she gets home, she can dress for the tropics.

We have another friend, Karen, who believes no matter what the season, if you are cold turn on the heat. If you are hot, turn on the air conditioner. There was a little cool spell back in late May? She turned on the heat because the temperatures had dropped to the high sixties. I remember when she was running her air conditioner during a little February warm spell of 72 degrees. "Jimmy Carter be damned," Karen said. In the winter the temperature should be 76 degrees in the house. In the summer, she sets the thermostat on 70. I cannot enter that house in the winter. I can't breathe because it is so hot. Snell, on the other hand, is very happy.

LIFE IS HARD SOFTEN IT WITH LAUGHTER

Karen also cusses Jimmy Carter when it is time to change the clocks. I have to agree with her on this one. That is a story for another day.

I woke up with three out of four cats and Snell all pressed up against me in the bed this morning. The fourth cat and James were huddled together under a fleece blanket. If the tip of Figaro's tail hadn't moved, I might not have found them. You know it is time to turn the heat on when felines and humans begin to seek heat from each other.

During the night, Snell had gotten up, put on his heaviest fleece pants, and crawled back into bed. The blanket was over his head when I looked at him this morning. The house was sixty-six degrees. I admit that my internal furnace runs a bit higher than anyone else's in the house, but I thought it was kind of nice and comfortable. I slept under just a sheet. Snell mumbled from under the blanket, sheet, bedspread, and three cats, "I think we need to change to a warmer bedspread." Hey, I gave him a light blanket a week or so ago. Now, he wants the 100-pound comforter that he says is too heavy and doesn't like.

So today, with the outside temperatures at fifty degrees and the inside a balmy sixty-six degrees. I turned on the heat, brought down the comforter, and made Snell very happy. He doesn't know how lucky he is. According to Margie, he has five more days before he can have the heat on.

Track and Field

Recently, I have felt like I have been on that continuous loop around the football field. I keep going, but I run back through my same steps again and again. The hurdles are placed at odd intervals, and they are not all the same height. The faster I run the more I trip and fall.

Do you feel this way sometimes? Are you running next to me?

What is going on, y'all? I am so maudlin today. I don't mean to be. It is my intent for this story up-lifting and make you laugh. Well, duh. I'm not doing such a good job.

Are you overwhelmed? Me, too. Why can't we get a grip on things? I have never seen so much disorganization in my life as it is now. Is there some type of disturbance in the universe that could be the reason? Hurricanes, eclipses, phases of the moon? I don't think so. I am just drowning in "things to do". Things that should have been done. Things other people want. LIFE!

The next person who asks me to do something for them just might get to watch full-blown temper tantrum in action And I don't mean one of those wishy-washy two-year- old jobs. Pitch it, cry, and it's over. I mean one that has been building for years. If anyone can pitch a hissy fit, it is an old woman who has had ENOUGH!

I am trying to visualize fat, elderly, little ol' me lying on the floor, kicking and screaming. Red faced and bawling. Totaling ineffective if I have to have someone come hoist me back up onto my feet. I need to practice getting up and down so this tantrum will be more effective and memorable. I promise you it will be memorable and not a pretty sight.

I am planning a tantrum that comes with lots of verbalizations. A kicking and screaming hissy fit with unbelievable gyrations. Language that will make sailors blush. Heart stopping whammy mammy fits. Frothing at the mouth, eyes rolling back in the head, and bottom lip stuck out at least three inches. One that comes with tons of resentment, weeks of poor sleep, months of stress, and the knowledge that this will be my only chance to really show-out.

Let me see that one in my mind..... Nope, I think that would only bring momentary relief and might alienate a few people. On the up side, I might get solitary confinement. Hey, maybe I could go in for just a little break. It would be nice to make a decision of only vertical or horizontal bars on my windows. I bet someone would even take that responsibility away from me. That might be okay. Well, maybe for a little while.

If I do, I would feel guilty because I have neglected all the people and animals that depend on me. Then, I wouldn't be sleeping again. The loop would still be there with all the uneven hurdles. Confined, I could do even less about them.

Well, crap.

Maybe I should have followed the advice I used to tell my students' parents when they couldn't stand all the adolescent angst in their house. I'd advise them to go into the bathroom with the following items: a pillow, a box of Kleenex and a twelve pack of Hershey bars. Once inside their fortress of refuge to lock the door, scream into the pillow, blow their nose and eat a Hershey bar. This procedure should be repeated as often as necessary.

Okay. Things are going to be better. It is darkest before the dawn. I have lived through worse.

Y'all, please excuse me. I need to get my pillow and Hershey bars. I have about an hour I need to spend in the bathroom.

Social Calendars

What does your social calendar look like? I have three calendars. One in my purse, one on the refrigerator, and one by the computer. When I worked, I had a fourth on my desk. Every event was color coordinated. Mama was purple, James was blue, Snell was green, animals were orange, and I was pink. If the entire household was involved, the event would be marked in yellow. Very colorful. It was sort of like an organized Jackson Pollock and, to me, a lot more valuable than any painting.

I remember when I had lots of blank spaces on my calendar boxes. I had names of people and events written in for evenings and weekends, but our calendar never runneth over. We had a social life. We went to festivals and art shows. We had a number of activities we enjoyed. I used to cook. We would invite people over for parties and dinner.

We had nice clothes we wore to go to places. We got dressed up and went out. Now, we have funeral finery. The only place we go that requires one to look nice is the funeral home. Of course, some people haven't gotten that message and show up looking like the morning after.

Now, I look at my calendar and think, "Where is the fun stuff?"

Each week, our son James does a photography class and a glass blowing class. He thoroughly enjoys them and he is good at both activities. Because he doesn't drive, we take him. Snell and I usually read and watch what James is making. After glass class, we occasionally go to a gluten-free bakery and have a dessert. We'd laugh and talk together as we swooned over some decadent sweet. That was probably the social highlight of our week.

I was looking over the remainder of this month and all of next month's calendar squares. I was hoping to fit in a lunch with some retired teachers when I realized something kind of sad.

Almost every square had something written in it. Not fun stuff, but doctor's appointments, termite people coming, duty and responsibility kind of things. So, I looked back at the earlier part of the month. That was more depressing.

I had filled in times and names of funerals we needed to attend around our scheduled events. Mama always said when the sap starts to rise (spring) or starts to fall (autumn), more deaths occur. She was right.

I have noticed how true her saying is when reading obituary columns. Oh, don't lie to me. You read them, too. It may not be the first thing you read, but you check out who died. And you compare your age to those who are listed. You feel short changed when the obituary includes only the minimum information. You want a complete listing of all the family members because you might know some of them. You want to know the cause of death, too. Do you swipe your hand across your forehead and go, "Whew. I didn't know anyone this time"? Or, "I wasn't on there today!"

I have found that our social life centers around funeral homes now. I see people only when someone dies. Sometimes, we go to dinner with someone after the funeral home visit, but even then, death was the gravitational force that brought us together.

Are we that old that we count our days by how many people we outlive? I am beginning to think so. I want the old life of art festivals and fun stuff, not all these "death events." I am making a change in our lives. Right after the funeral Thursday, I am going to plan something fun.

The Other Side of Laughter

"Life is hard. Sometimes it is hard to find the laughter."

Noah's Ark

I have to tell you about James, Sunday School, and church. We used to go to church regularly. Because of James' disability, he has always slept at least twelve hours. It takes a lot of energy for him to stay focused and that was why he needed that much sleep. James enjoyed Sunday School so much he would get up early on Sundays. He was ready to go!

James would head right for his class and frequently be the first one there. He had such great husband-wife team of teachers. In the middle of the term, his teachers changed, and he got a new woman who was not tolerate of James in the least little bit.

I remember vividly the story of James, the teacher, and Noah's Ark. My daddy could make about anything you could think of from wood. He had created James an ark, and they played with it a lot. It was big, and James used his plastic animals with it. According to James, unicorns and dinosaurs all made it aboard the ark. It was his favorite story.

His second favorite was Daniel and Lion's Den. Daddy would be Daniel and talk to the animals. James would be the lions, tigers, bears, and maybe a dinosaur or two. This poor Daniel faced a lot more than a couple of hungry lions!!

LIFE IS HARD SOFTEN IT WITH LAUGHTER

When James started being reluctant to go to Sunday School, we couldn't figure out why. He had always been so enthusiastic that he could hardly wait to get there. He was making some friends in the class, too. He was talking about them and the things they studied. We would do our own little lesson on whatever the theme was for the next week. Maybe, that was a mistake. Maybe, he knew too much about the topic before class.

We had bought him the Hanna-Barbera Bible Stories, too. He loved them. He would watch them and tell us about it. Snell's Aunt Kate DeLoach (Aunt Cake) was living in the little house next door, and she and James visited often. Aunt Kate could recite the Bible forward and backward, but she wasn't a Bible thumper. She knew it, and she lived it. She and James had discussions about the Bible stories that she told him.

Anyway, this new Sunday School teacher was very rigid. How can you be rigid with a bunch of kindergarteners? And with Bible stories? We had tried several times to talk to her about James' new reluctance to attend. She didn't call us back and never had time for us. She was always in a rush after the class ended. We didn't think these were good teaching practices.

One day, Snell and I left our Sunday School class early and went to stand outside of his classroom. On this particular day, Noah's Ark was the lesson. We heard James answer a question, and she responded. "Sit down, James. I will call on you when I want to hear from you." Her voice was really harsh. I swear that was what she said. Oh, dear. Snell and I looked at each other.

James was the only special needs kid in the class, and maybe she didn't understand how impulsive he could be. We had met with her briefly when she took over the class. We always made sure his teachers knew about James' special needs. We thought it was important that his teachers know about his incredible knowledge and his severe ADHD and poor speech.

When class was over, we asked if she had a minute to talk. She said she had only a minute and had to get the classroom straightened up. She never had a minute after class to talk. We had heard her tell the kids to stand up, put their chairs in place, and return everything to the cabinet. The classroom was spotless.

Snell asked her how James was doing and if he was participating well. She let us have it. James was a troublemaker. He did not always raise his hand and wanted to answer all the questions. Sometimes, he talked out loud. He liked to stand while they colored and not sit down. She went on and on. James couldn't do anything right for her. She thought he should be out of her class. That was one thing we all found ourselves in agreement.

We tried to find him another class, but there wasn't one. We were told there were not enough teachers. I offered to teach a class if he could be placed with someone besides me or the current teacher. No was the answer I received. I was disappointed in their response to try to help us with this issue.

So, after the Noah's Ark incident and James begging to not go to Sunday School, we stopped. We went to church, but not Sunday School. Then he got to where he wanted to go for only special events. Soon, he wouldn't go at all if he could help it. The idea of going to church was so stressful that he would cry if we tried to get him to go with us. It went from his favorite thing to his least favorite thing.

He still has his cartoon Bible stories from all those years ago. Every once in a while, I will be upstairs and hear him playing them. Sometimes Snell and I go to Sunday School and leave James at home. I feel bad doing that. Now that he is older, I have offered him other options of changing churches or going to different Sunday School classes. "No. I used to like it. I don't, now."

LIFE IS HARD SOFTEN IT WITH LAUGHTER

I know this isn't funny, but it is important that we all be reminded that tolerance for difference is a very important thing. Kermit the Frog said, "It isn't easy being green." Well, he's right. It isn't easy being unique.

Goodbye Dear Friend

I am grieving over the loss of a dear friend, The Big Tree. That is what we called her. The Big Tree.

We had an old, old oak beside our sunroom. We placed the house and the sunroom, so The Big Tree was a focus for our lives.

Irma murdered her.

We kept The Big Tree happy and healthy with visits from the tree doctor every five years. She got fertilizer regularly, and during the drought we gave her as much water as we could. She has been an anchor on this land for around 300 years.

Ten years ago, an Atlanta arborist was running a contest through metro-Atlanta. They were trying to identify as many of the old trees and to determine which were the largest. We submitted The Big Tree, and she was identified as the second largest post oak in the area. I had planned to enter her in the study again this year.

This summer, our son James and I measured her waist at five feet above ground level. She was about seventeen feet in circumference. She was solid, too. So many old trees develop a hollow core, but not the Big Tree. She was heart all the way through.

I positioned my work table in the sunroom to face The Big Tree. Every morning, I watched our two hawks fly around the yard. One always lit on the large limb that comes forward and to the right. We had a squirrel with a white tip on its tail that visited. He played on The Big Tree every morning. He and the hawks must have had an agreement. The squirrel played on the left side of the tree and the hawk sat on the right. Birds often occupied the limbs and were a constant source of entertainment. I LIKED to think we said our good mornings to each other through the window. The Big Tree and all the critters and I had visited in this manner for over twenty-two years.

Mama's murder of crows, Geraldine, Vincent, and Edgar walked around under The Big Tree and sat in its huge branches. I fed them there sometimes. They would sit in the tree and wait for one of us to come out of the house with their supper. We called their names. Geraldine answered, and in they all swooped.

Years ago, we had found this property through the Farmer's Market Bulletin. I think it was love at first sight. On it were a water fall and two post oaks. One tree was badly diseased and had a hollow core. We experienced bad winds from Hurricane Opal in 1995, and those winds split the diseased tree. But The Big Tree just stood there proudly and said, "I'm still here for you."

James made her part of his photography class project. We planted tulips, irises, day lilies, and money plants under her limbs. She had beautiful feet when those flowers were in bloom. Mama and Daddy had a metal swing for as long as I can remember. That swing went to every new house when they moved. The last action of moving Mama from their home was to place the swing under The Big Tree.

The Big Tree anchored our home in so many ways. This morning, I looked at the huge root structure exposed to world. It is rather unseemly somehow to have her skirts up in the air like that. Her broken limbs look like shattered ribs, and her arms are splayed on the ground. The hawk flew around her, looking down at the remains. Finally, she landed on one of the huge branches reaching up to the sky. I guess she was saying goodbye, too.

I am trying to find wood craftsmen and artists who would like to preserve The Big Tree in some sort of beautiful way. I just can't see her gorgeous, sturdy body destroyed. It needs to become works of art in tribute to the work of art she was.

Irma tore up a lot of things and did a lot of damage in a lot of places, and during her angry attack on our town, she tore a hole in my heart.

A Peaceful Place

I do a lot of funerals. Earlier in our lives together, Snell and I went to funerals together. I ended up sitting alone because most of the times he was a pall bearer. One of his cousins, Margaret Snell Gilbert, was a widow. Margaret and I became funeral friends, best buddies in bye-byes. We didn't see each other outside of funerals and funeral homes, but we could find each other in a crowd. We were magnetized like that. When Margaret died, I felt like I was supposed to be sitting next to her casket. One last funeral together.

This week, I went to only one funeral. The woman who died was the mother of one of my high school classmates. I was running way late because of poor planning on my part and heavy traffic. I made it to A.S. Turner's in Decatur with only a few minutes to spare. I slipped into the chapel and saw Bruce Garner, an old classmate of mine. We visited for just a few minutes before the service started.

I was again taken by the beauty of Turner's chapel. For several years, there were fish tanks outside the chapel. I remember as a child watching the fish and later as an adult, doing the same thing. They were beautiful, mesmerizing, calming and took your mind away from why you were there.

Inside the chapel is pretty and calming too. The beautiful woods and the lighting fixtures are lovely. What takes my breath away every time I visit Turners is the stained glass. It is not of a religious depiction, but instead are sweeping colors. The curves and banding of colors are clear and shaped so that you feel upward bound, for lack of a better description.

Newer funeral home chapels don't have the beauty that Turner's has. They are functional and well decorated. I have visited a lot of them and I will always say the chapels serve their purpose well, and with grace and loveliness.

There is just something about Turner's chapel that feels right. I am sure I am sitting with a lot of ghosts and many good and bad memories have passed through.

A Place for Little Souls

G rowing up, my family always had animals. I had cats, chickens, dogs, rabbits, squirrels, fish, and birds living in the house. The rabbit used the potty box along with the cats. It was no surprise that Mama would take in a stray cat when she moved into the Little House in our front yard.

Mama's little Peppy passed on recently. Mama took Peppy in fifteen years ago. The vet told us she was probably two or three years old at that time. She had had at least one litter of kittens.

Originally, Mama had named her Rosalind. When she found out that Rosalind belonged to the family next door and was called Peppy, she reluctantly began calling her Peppy.

Mama worked in the yard a few hours every morning and again in the late afternoon. Peppy would meet her at the kitchen door, and they would spend all day together. Peppy sat next to Mama on the wrought iron furniture or the little bench and visited while they rested. They had long philosophical conversations. Peppy told Mama how much she loved bacon, and Mama cooked her a piece every morning with a little scrambled egg. Most days they had lunch together by the fire pit.

One day, it was very cold. We had ice forming on the trees and ground. Mama fixed the garage with a heater, a box with towels, and a pillow in it. She wanted Peppy to

101

stay with her and not go home in the cold. She got Peppy settled in the warm garage with her snuggly place and a nice dinner.

Concerned that her neighbors might worry about Peppy not being able to make it home in the bad weather, Mama called them to let them know that Peppy was all right and would be spending the night in her heated garage. The neighbor informed Mama that they hadn't seen "that cat" since they had her fixed.

Mama went back outside, opened the garage door, and Peppy came in the house, where she lived for the rest of her life. Mama fixed her one piece of bacon and they shared a scrambled egg together most mornings for the next ten years until Mama passed away. We went every day to spend time with Peppy, but she mourned Mama. She wouldn't eat her bacon any more.

Cyndi, a former Parkview student of mine and colleague from our teaching days at Central Gwinnett, moved into Mama's house. The deal was, you get to live in Mama's house with Peppy IF Peppy accepts you. I had to promise Mama that Peppy would be cared for the remainder of her life. Cyndi, God love her, is an animal person, too. She and Peppy found happiness together. The bond was there from the minute Cyndi walked into the Little House. I am sure Mama was putting super glue on them both, because they stuck together.

Peppy was at least sixteen years old when she passed. We buried her in the family plot with the rest of our babies. Our little dog, Puddles, died in 1994, before the house was built. He loved to lie in the shade of a couple of cedar trees on the hill above the future house site. It was Puddles who determined our family cemetery. We moved the grave stones from Mama and Daddy's house on Vera Cruz to this new cemetery site. Over the years, we have had to add new graves. Keenan Byrd has the blueprint for all of our tombstones. I just send him the information, and he brings us the head stone.

Cyndi could not live without another animal to look after. The story continues with these two cats that had been hanging around the house. They sat in the window and talked with Peppy through the breakfast room window screen. Peppy was frail and couldn't go outside anymore, but she could have the fresh air and visits from Mama Kitty and Bolden. They had been circling the little house and our house for a while. Both Cyndi and we fed them. We talked to them regularly, but neither would let us touch them. I think having the four feline hoodlums glowering from our windows was intimidating.

Cyndi, on the other hand, was a cat whisperer. They found a kindred spirit in her and in Peppy's left over food dish. After some time, the fluffy little boy, Bolden, was sick and got to stay in the laundry room to recover. He decided he really liked indoor living. He had camped out long enough. At his first opportunity, he moved in with Cyndi and Peppy.

The solid grey, Mama Kitty had been with us for a long time. About four or five years ago, we caught her and all of her kittens. They were put out of the baby making business as fast as we could drive them to the vet's office. We gave her and all of the babies to Snell's cousins, Peggy and Steven. As soon as Peggy, Steven, and their neighbors, who divided the pride of cats, let them out, the cats scooted into the woods. On occasion, you might see a grey streak running through the woods behind their houses. However, Mama Kitty came home.

Mama Kitty started making eyes at Cyndi. After all, Cyndi was putting out food and spending time with her outside. Of course, Mama Kitty ate at our house and at Cyndi's. As she and Bolden began to get friendly, share food, and not fuss at one another, they began to plot moving into the Little House.

THEN, Sly came up from the creek. Sly was sly. He was originally named TDH for Tall, Dark, and Handsome. A beautiful tuxedo cat, he looked like he would be a lover, but apparently, he was a fighter. Sly stared Mama Kitty and Bolden down until they moved away from their food and then he moved in to eat it all. Sly has beaten the crap out of both Bolden and Mama Kitty on more than one occasion and taught them to be very fearful of him. Cyndi started letting Mama Kitty and Bolden come in to eat.

Cyndi is THE ONLY ONE who can get even a little close to Mama Kitty, who is so nervous around others. Feral for more than five years, Mama Kitty has only had contact with us from a distance. Trust me, James and I have tried to win her over. Only Cyndi has been successful.

Mama Kitty and Bolden have talked Cyndi into needing them both in her life and in her house. Snell, James, and I had talked about how long it would take before they both moved in permanently. Both cats lived in the house with Cyndi after Peppy died. Neither cat had made any attempt to approach the door and return to living outside. They knew a good thing, and they were not going to jeopardize having to rough it any more.

So, I salute you, Cyndi. You were no stronger than the rest of us when it comes to lost souls and needy waifs. I was proud to have you as part of the Cat House family. You were a perfect fit. Peppy knew it from the first moment she met you.

Cats

"I have flying monkeys, and I'm not afraid to use them."
Wicked Witch of Oz

The Invasion of the Flying Monkeys.

Our son, James, called me from work the other day to tell me about two kittens he had found hiding under the trash compactor. I wish I could have five minutes with the Sweet Old Boy/Biddie who threw those kittens out into a parking lot.

If there is a lost animal or an injured soul, James is going to find it. Apparently, we are waif collectors. We have critters who find us—two legged, three legged, and four legged kinds.

When James called, I knew immediately we were about to be back in the kitten business. This called for swift action on my part. My first task was advising James to ask all of his ladies at work if they would take them. My second was to enlist back-up through James' supervisor with the request of an email sent to everyone at the school, asking if anyone would be willing to adopt the kittens.

My next move was to call everyone I knew, including every vet's office around the Snellville, Loganville, and Grayson area. No luck there. The next list of possible new kitten parents was the beauty shop, my dentist office, every contact on my email list, and anyone who owed me a favor. NO ONE would take them. I know a lot of people, too. At this point, the idea to start revoking

some high school diplomas was sounding like a solid
plan. Trust me, I have secrets and stories that could be
detrimental to many careers.

Well, the kittens became the newest members of our
family despite all my threats and efforts. Did I really
expect this situation to turn out any differently?

They have been named Figaro and Mystic. Figaro
turns out to have "freckles" that are appropriate for her
to be misidentified as a male. These freckles caused her
to have received a male name, but she is a little girl. She
had her first gynecological exam to prove it. Figaro is a
smart even tempered little grey tiger. Mystic is black and
white with almost ying/yang face markings. She should
have been named Tasmanian Devil, Hell on Wheels, Evil
Catnevil, or LuciFUR! Perhaps Destructor would be best.
I have lost a lot of my dust catchers to that one.

The little things weighed less than 2 ½ pounds each
and were around six to eight weeks old when James
brought them home. At first, we couldn't keep enough
food in front of them. They were like little Hoover
Vacuum cleaners, just sucking up the food and water.
The kittens were so starved they actually ate three cans
of kitten food within three hours. Both have doubled in
weight and size within the last month.

Ramona has been the only cat in the house since our
Miss Molly died last winter. Ramona inhaled a bot fly
larva that left her brain injured. She is still weak,
visually impaired, and needs help finding her food at
times. She is used to being waited on hand and paw, her
reward as the poor, pitiful, injured Queen Pussycat.

Every once in a while, Ramona will see one of the
babies, and she will just stare at it. I don't think she
knows what to do with a kitten, and I don't think she
wants to learn. She looks at the two kittens and then up
at Snell. You can read her mind. "What are those things?
Do I want them? No, I don't think so. Daddy, pick me
up."

Mystic thinks Ramona is her Mama, but Ramona
knows she isn't. Mystic wants to play with Ramona's

tail, but Ramona's tail is not up for grabs. We know Ramona's strength and coordination is improving. It was very evident when Mystic grabbed her tail. Ramona slapped Mystic in the face fifteen times in two seconds before turning around and stomping off to another location. She stomped off. No little pussy footsteps taken.

We have never had small kittens. Every other critter showed up fully grown and in need. Ramona was about five or six months old when we found her. Miss Molly was several years old when she found us. I didn't have to baby proof the house but having these two is much like when James was learning to walk. These critters are like flying monkeys. I expect to see the Wicked Witch of the West drop in at any moment. These cats don't walk. They jump from one piece of furniture to another. They levitate themselves straight up in the air so that I feel like Winnie the Pooh's Tigger lives/leaps here.

Cat fights and Live Atlanta Wrestling are very much alike. Figaro and Mystic sit peacefully like Meer Cats on their haunches, and then they will start to grab and fight with one another. If they didn't have fur, you would see black and blue marks all over them.

One of their moves is the Godzilla Death Grip. They start out doing a Meer Cat face off and then they grab one another, weaving back and forth in a death battle on the couch. They never release one another until they fall off the couch onto their heads. I swear to you, Ramona snickered at that.

The Fur Balls of Death

We have four cats, all were rescues, and none are touchy feely. I really wanted a cat that was like my little Ramona. She loved to be held and combed or to sit with you. She'd wrapped herself around my neck and ride on my shoulders wherever I was walking. These four in residence now were never truly socialized as babies, so they have made up their own rules. They will let us pet them if they come to us, but they will not get into our laps and be loved. Combed yes, in their designated combing stations. Figaro sleeps on James' bed in her spot, but she won't sleep touching him.

Figaro, AKA the Queen, has us all well trained. We know if she comes up to one of us in the kitchen, stands on her back feet, and rubs against one's leg it means "Moo. I want my mini-moo." Mini-moos are those individual half and half coffee creamers. We have to go through a ritual with her. We all do it while using our sing-songy baby talk voices. Lord, help us. Rubbing between her "eyebrows" and asking "Do you want a moo? How many moos do you want? Is it a one moo morning or a two-moo morning?" Yeah, don't call anyone. The psychiatrist already knows we are nuts or cat-a-tonic. Oh, stop groaning. The pun wasn't that bad.

Periodically, we buy things for the cats thinking they will play with us, but they are just new toys to ignore. Although, the laser light was a hit. We keep scratching posts and pads around to distract them from the furniture. We treat the scratch pads with catnip to make them more inviting. I do not treat my grandmother's sofa with catnip, but that is their favorite scratching place. Everything in the house is covered with sheets or towels. I try to explain to visitors that cat fur is a protective agent for hardwood floors and upholstered furniture. No one buys my theory, and they look at me with pity for trying to justify the fur tumbleweeds.

Back to the story. I bought the cats a new scratching pad and it is elevated--like a launch pad. It has a little stick with yellow feathered fluff at the peak of the pad. Gracie loves it. So far, we have glued the feathers back on twice.

This morning, I was in the kitchen cleaning up and doing some odd and end jobs when I heard a screech and saw a black fur ball fly through the air. Both Mystic and Gracie have a lot of black on them so I don't know which one was doing the aerial assault on the other one. Lots of noise and then they did a streak or two through the house. My poor fraidey cat, Samson, was scared to death and trying to hide.

The flying black and white ball landed on another black and white ball and the two become one, rolling over the entire kitchen and den in blood curdling screams. I was frozen in place. I didn't know who, what, or where the balls were. I just knew death and mayhem were in the air.

About that time, I saw the ball break apart and Mystic (more white than black) race toward the bedroom. Gracie (more black than white) was in hot pursuit. Samson (all black and a scardy cat) came around the corner of the door on only his right paws. He looked at me in frightened wonder and disappeared under a couch.

A moment later, Gracie exited the bedroom at 120 mph, and Mystic followed her at breakneck speed. Suddenly, there was that screech again, and Gracie flew off the end of the launching pad and cleared at least three feet of air. Mystic was waiting, standing on her back feet, arms outstretched as if to catch Gracie when wham! Gracie slammed into Mystic's chest. Mystic's arms and legs encased Gracie in a choke hold, and they started that deadly roll again. One of the lamps started to shake, and the camera alarm recorder hit the floor. Black and white fur flew around the room. I was waiting for blood and guts or a dead cat or both. They slammed into the couch where poor scared Samson was hiding. He scooted out, trying in vain to run for all he is worth to another room. Because his feet are furry, he can't get a grip, so he is slippin' and slidin' all over the floor. Without traction, he wasn't going anywhere, just a black fluff wad with little legs running in place. His green eyes were huge and pleading. "Save me, Mama. Save me!"

SLAM! The black fur ball of death and destruction hit the legs of the telephone table. The vase with the pens and pencils shake, rattle, and spill all over the floor. The pad of paper hit the floor and broke apart, paper with little flowers showering around the fur ball of mass destruction. The black fur ball rolled itself on into the sunroom, slamming into doors, chairs, and everything possible to hit. Philodendron leaves were ripped off the vines in the struggle for survival. Wham! The cats knock on the door to the bathroom and landed in the middle of the floor where they stopped. Just stopped. They are not even breathing hard. Mystic casually walked over and washed Gracie's' face. Gracie did the same thing for Mystic, and then they strolled off together into the other room.

A time lapse of maybe two minutes had occurred. I was left cleaning up paper, pens, and plant leaves while they calmly nibbled their crunchies. Samson had gone into a catatonic stupor and was not be seen for hours. Figaro walked in, took one look around, turned, and flicked her tail. (I really think that is a cat's way of giving the world the middle finger.) She went into James' room and lay on his bed, too elite to be troubled by the gladiators who had turned our house into the Colosseum of War.

The Revenge of the Disgruntled Cats

We got the message: Don't ever go away again! Yes, we made a mistake. We actually thought we could take a vacation, return home, and the cats would be OK. Didn't happen.

Our friend Cyndi took good care of the livestock. She fed them, visited, and played with them daily. They were all a little feral when they came to live with us. Except for Samson, who was emotionally and behaviorally disturbed. None of them were very cuddly. The closest you got to a cuddle was at the vet's office when they are trying to hide behind you.

We got in about 12:45 AM. We were tired, and all we wanted to do was be out of a moving vehicle. The cats all came out of their various hiding places and looked at us. Not one welcomed us home. Not one let us pet her or him. Eventually, Figaro came closer and smelled of Snell's shoes. I guess that was the signal. Everyone else was sort of OK, but Gracie didn't have anything to do with us until the next morning, though.

They were going to get us for being gone. I could tell. I walked in and Samson, I know it was him, had peed outside the box. At least, he had urinated on the puppy pads. He likes to do that to punish us. While I cleaned up his act of defiance, he fluffed his tail as if to say, "There's more."

I swear to you each cat managed to throw up at least once for every day we were gone. They did not miss a room in the whole house. I believe Mystic can vomit at will. If she believes she has been wronged, she will just barf all that aggravation and irritation up and not care where it lands. Thank goodness all the rooms upstairs were closed. They have carpeting.

About 1:30 AM, I am still rocking and rolling from the ship and travel exhaustion. I am thinking "bed" when Snell says, "What's that?" Mystic had thrown up all over the window, window sill, down the wall, and on top of my Aunt Hazel's sewing cabinet. I know it had to be her because the window was Mystic's favorite place to sit and stare at the outside world. She had jumped up onto the cedar chest and was smiling at me. I could hear her "nannie-nannie-poo-poohing" at me.

Just when I thought I had cleaned every spot of cat barf, James yells, "Mom. Somebody went to the bathroom in my bathroom." Yep, I am pretty sure it was Samson, again. James had stepped right in a pile on his bathroom rug. I swear to you, I heard snickering from under the bed.

We got the message from the cats. "Don't ever go away again!"

In the vain hope they would appreciate/forgive us, I got up the next morning and fed them tuna, which gags me to smell. The pride of cats was still standoffish, but they did eat. Snell left to go get the top of his head cut off at the dermatologist, and I took James to work. When I got home, I cleaned up the cats' tuna-scented throw-up.

AH, home.

Mystic and the Possum

A bout 1:30 this morning, I woke up to a clicking noise. It was rhythmic and near the bed. I lay there trying to figure it out. It wasn't hail or water dropping. I sat up, and Mystic, our black and white cat, was on the back of an old Morris chair that sits by a window.

Mystic was intently watching something, patting, and scratching at the window glass. Periodically, she would turn her head and look at me. "Get over here. See this? Come on, Mama, get this for me."

I reluctantly got up and went to her. We both looked out the window. I couldn't see anything. Nothing. I thought maybe Mystic was having a lunacy moment. Then, something pale moved. Mystic looked up at me as if to say, "See! There it is. What is it? I want it. I don't know what it is, but I want it. Give it to me! NOW!"

I still couldn't see it well enough to determine what it was. It was just something pale and, for all I could tell, might have been a leaf shifting in the moonlight. She and I went to the laundry room. Mystic on to the washing machine and then to the dryer so she could sit on the window ledge. Again, she looked at me with that demanding face. I couldn't see out that window. I left Mystic sitting on the window ledge and put on shoes. I crept out into the garage to the doors that open into the back yard. I still could only see a hazy, pale colored, little ball, and it wasn't moving anymore.

I thought it might be a kitten. I opened the door and walked outside where I could see it better. It was a small possum. It looked at me, I looked at it, and Mystic looked at both of us from the laundry room window. The possum ran. I gave out a sigh relief that it wasn't a kitten, but Mystic glared at me. "You let it get away. It is mine. Go get it."

Mystic and I went back to bed. I tried to explain to her that she couldn't have it. She didn't believe me. I told her it was a baby possum, and it had to live outside. Oh, no. She was mad. She punished me for the rest of the night. She would watch out the window, come stand on me and stare down. I could hear her little brain whirling "You let it go. Go get it. Bring it back. I want my new pet. It is all your fault."

Curiosity Sticks the Cat

Remember our two flying monkeys, Figaro and Mystic? They don't seem to be flying so high anymore! They seem to be doing more pussy footing instead.

We started a remodeling project last year that included a new laundry room and some changes to the old laundry room. What seemed like an easy project became wrapped in the whirlwind of our lives. We finally were able to place cabinets in the old laundry room.

Snell and his cousin, Charles, installed the new cabinets. They were a beautiful snowy white and just brightened up the entire room. Plus, I really needed the storage space. It didn't take long to fill up the drawers with junk that should have been tossed.

You know how curious cats can be. Figaro and Mystic were in every drawer and every cabinet. They had an active part in all the installation processes. Before I could put liner paper in the drawers and on the shelves, there was cat hair in each drawer. I am pretty sure I collected enough fur to make another whole cat.

The idea to use the same tile from the floor as the counter top seemed like a good one and I asked Snell and Charles if they would lay the tile. I know how they were always willing to do anything I ask. You believe that? They'll do anything that kept me from whining and fussing.

They spread the glue on the counter top and went to accomplish another important task-lunch. The glue needed to cure to a specific consistency before the tiles could be placed. An hour was enough time for this process.

Curiosity sticks the cat. I don't know who was first on the countertop, but she slid from one end to other in that glue. Pussy foot prints were everywhere. Two sets of them and we could track the prints into every room of the house.

You know how cats will shake their feet when they get wet? Eight feet going every which way, throwing globules of glue on the walls, on the floor, on the new snowy white cabinets. We caught Figaro on my Grandmother's couch in the living room. Yes, permanently autographed with Figaro's signature paw prints.

Nancy Smith Meek, a former teacher from Parkview and Phoenix High Schools and longtime friend had dropped by the house. "Welcome to my home, first time visitor. Hold this cat, paws out please. WE have to wash her feet and legs."

Nancy and I had been co-workers and friends for over thirty-five years. I knew she could handle anything. I should know. I chose a lot of kids to go into her classes because she was an excellent teacher and related well to all kinds of students. Nancy was a trouper and thought nothing of taking a very unhappy Mystic. James had managed to stalk down Figaro.

I must tell you there was a lot of foul language being used. Most of it was by the cats.

I tried Vaseline and cold cream to soften the glue. I think that might have made it set harder. Finally, I was soaking their feet in straight Dawn dishwashing liquid. I used 12 wash cloths to lather those eight sticky feet. Twelve more were used to remove the soap and glue. I guess out of sheer desperation, they stopped struggling and spread their toes so I could scrub their feet and work my way up their legs. I thought I would never get all that glue off, and all the time I am scrubbing Nancy and James were holding these two angry, frightened wiggle worms.

There we were with two very unhappy, sticky and soapy cats. We finally removed most of the soap and glue. Then we attempted to powder their feet with corn starch to soak up the water and glue residue. Don't do that. Then we tried to dry them with towels. Yeah, they weren't thrilled with that idea either. James suggested we use the hair dryer. I told him that we had been in the emergency room enough this year. Thank you very much.

Once down on the floor the cats began dancing the Pussy Footing Hokey Pokey. You put your left paw out and you shake it all about. At one time, Figaro was doing the advanced "Dancing with the Stars" version – put your left paw out and your back right foot out and shake them all about. I really don't know how she remained standing. Poor Mystic was dancing around. She finally collapsed on the rug with all four feet straight up in the air. She spread her toes and shooked her feet.

I don't know where those kittens learned their language. They do have an extensive and quite colorful vocabulary. It must have been from being around lower-class cats before we found them. They were thrown out at a trash compactor/dumpster. I am sure they didn't learn all of those words from us.

Do you know what happens when you wash kitty feet with Dawn and you don't get all the soap off? Well, James swore he saw soap suds in the potty box the next morning! And Nancy has never come back to my house.

MARLENE RATLEDGE BUCHANAN

It was One of those Mornings.

H ave you ever had "one of those mornings" where everything you touched turned to mud? The best thing you could say was that you lived through it. This was one of those "quantity of life and not quality of life" days.

At 3:10 in the morning a cat threw-up. I wasn't sure where it was so in my unerring way, my bare foot found it for me. She must have been saving up. As fast as one spot was cleaned, she could be heard in another room doing the yack and heave routine. By the time she had finished throwing up her guts most of the house had been hand mopped with Windex and paper towels. Do you remember the song "Oh, What a Beautiful Morning"? I was not singing that.

I went back to bed. And there I lay. Closing my eyes only allowed all of those things floating around in my brain to surface. How had I managed to become responsible for so many people and so much stuff? At 4:40, I decided the cat probably ate the Sandman and that was fairy guts I had been cleaning up. I might as well get up and do something.

All of these rescue cats James had brought home were not the kind that ran to sit in your lap. They expected you to wait on them. They didn't cuddle. The only time I could find all four of them was when I popped the top on a can of cat food. It sounded like a herd of horses racing to the kitchen. The deal was I start

120

a cup of coffee in the microwave and began a fresh pot perking. I would feed the hairball producing little souls. By the time the potty boxes were clean, they were finishing eating and were nowhere to be seen.

The three that usually slept in our room had decided that even though it was the middle of the night, they wanted to be fed. They had three more hours before they had to be up and start the day, but if I was up, they wanted breakfast. Those three went so far as to get the fourth cat up. Figaro slept in the bed with our son. She was the Queen and did not lower herself to bed down with the peons. I was trying to be quiet so Snell and James could continue to sleep. It was a perfect morning to steal a little "me-time". You know: have a cup of coffee or three, sit in the quiet, answer emails, and maybe write a little bit.

I decided the herd could wait for breakfast. That way I wouldn't make any noise. I took a deep breath, a sip of coffee, and thought "This is nice. I haven't had a moment like this in a long time."

Suddenly I realized I didn't see a single cat. That didn't really worry me. I thought maybe they went back to bed, sulking because breakfast had not been served. No, they had united to create turmoil and beastly noises. One of the cats began to walk and sing. She was going all around the house yodeling. Two of them decided they would have a Gladiator and the Lion battle throughout the entire house. They were running and attacking each other, screaming the most ungodly sounds. The fourth one threw up. Sigh. It was 5:56 am. Snell and James didn't flinch. Trying to let them sleep was resulting in my nerves being shattered.

Neither Snell nor James lost a wink of sleep. I was trying to do something nice for them by being quiet and instead Armageddon ran rampant throughout the house. I think the Four Horsemen came through disguised as cats. They certainly sounded like Clydesdales clomping through the house. It was better to just feed the little blighters than have to deal with the repercussions.

121

Through all the cacophony of cat noise, neither one of my boys opened an eye.

I was determined to accomplish something for me that morning. One cup of coffee and a banana down, I attempted to take my four pounds of medicine. I opened my medicine box and proceeded to drop at least three pills. One went down the sink drain. Two hit the floor. Of course, the pills were white. The floor was white. My language was not white. Snell and James slept on as I crawled around and found two tablets. The hell with the five-second rule. I blew the cat fur off of them and swallowed. Whatever went down the drain probably wasn't something I really needed today. Hopefully, it wasn't my anti-homicidal pill.

I managed to knock over my second cup of coffee breaking the handle off the cup. Does anyone have a complete set of matching coffee mugs? I had three of one kind and five of another. There was one cup I used at Parkview High School for ten years. It was a "belly-washer" mug. It held about eighteen ounces. I could fill it up in the morning, let it sit on the cup heater all day until it made syrup. It never broke until I dropped it unpacking my office stuff when I retired. I needed to write an "Ode to my Coffee Cup." It was a dear old friend.

Having finally gotten that pride of wild cats fed and cleaned up all of the messes, I sat down with my third cup of coffee to stare at the computer screen. My computers were always named Hissy Prissy. There is a story there. Needless to say, Hissy was not always cooperative. This morning, she was raring to go. If I could only get going. I had typed the date on the screen. "What was that story line I had had in my feeble little brain only minutes ago?" It was gone. Vanished.

Okay, the third mug of coffee down and a review of my idea list, I could not accomplish a short story or an observation. It was 6: 52. I had poured my fourth cup of coffee. Each eight-ounce mug of coffee equaled at least two trips to the bathroom for a coffee deposit. Guess how I made my 10,000 steps a day.

I finally decided I would write this story you are now reading. I was making more typographical errors than I could count. My fingers and my brain were no longer connected, but I was typing away. I hoped your morning started off better than mine. The alarms had begun their shrieks and the boys were beginning to rouse from their slumber. It was 8 AM. I was exhausted, on a coffee buzz and I pretty sure that was my anti-homicidal pill that went down the drain.

How Could You Do That to Us

"**M**ama. Mama. Look!" Gracie implored. "What is it? It moves, Mama. Can I have it?"
Gracie was the baby of the family. She was a delicately boned little black and white Tuxedo cat. More tux than white shirt. She was a short-haired beauty whose fur gleamed blue black. She tended to open her roundish yellow eyes very widely and look innocent. Trust me. It was all a trick. Gracie was talking in her little "nik, nik" voice and staring at the side yard. I looked. By this time, Mystic and Samson had come to the window to check out Gracie's excitement.

At first, I thought we had a skunk. There was a blond curled tail bobbing along between two fallen limbs of the The Big Tree. It was stopping and starting, but at no time was more than the fluffy tail visible.

Now Figaro, THE Queen, had come up and was sitting with the other three. "Well, Mama, what are you going to do? Just stand there? Go find out if it is something we want." (I can interpret snide and snippy cat remarks very well.)

We all went to the front door. They sat there waiting for me to investigate. This, in itself, was extraordinary. All four of our cats are rescues, and we know that some of them had some hard times before we found them. (Excuse me, they found us.) Usually, when the door would open, Samson and Gracie would go into hiding. I think they are afraid someone will make them go outside again. You can just hear their little brains whirring, "Been there. Done that. Ain't doing it again!"

I stepped on the porch. About that time, the bobbing tail of the supposed skunk came out into plain view. It was a miniature Pomeranian. "Are you lost?" I called to the dog. It looked up and flew to me. It wanted to be picked-up. So, I lifted it and cradled it in my arms. Of course, it had been raining and the dog was soppy wet. Now both of us were wet as frogs. The little dog seemed to feel that he couldn't get close enough or be held tightly enough.

I had to turn around and face my formidable felines. They just--looked. Mystic, mostly white with black, was the motherly cat. She was standing with her front paws on the glass of the door. She was our Miss Curiosity. She couldn't wait to see what I had.

I opened the door to come in. All four cats looked-up. They then stood, and in unison walked me and "that thing" in my arms to the kitchen. Synchronized swimmers couldn't have done a better job.

I grabbed a kitchen towel and tried to dry up some of the water from the little wiggle worm. Of course, today I was wearing dress clothes, not jeans or yard work clothes. The good stuff. The whole house smelled like wet dog.

All four cats were standing around me looking at the dog. Figaro stood on her hind legs and I leaned over for her to get a better view of the fluff of fur in my arms.

OOH! Mistake. Figaro, who was not only our Lord and Master, but was also the smart one in the bunch, went, "Dang! DOG." She twitched her tail and turned to the others. "Mama has a DOG. A D-O-G." Suddenly there was nothing but a whirlwind of cat fluff in the air. I didn't see a cat anywhere. It was just me and Stinky. Both damp and alone in the kitchen.

I continued to mop up some of the water off the little dog, calling it by every name I could think of. "Puppy, Roscoe, Bogart, Baby, Randolph, Fido, Rover, Dust

Devil." It was obviously a little boy, but no attempts to guess his name worked.

I brought him into the sunroom where I could close all the doors and finish drying him and myself. We had a physical therapy pool in this room. And you know it before I tell you. As soon as I put him down, he went running around and jumped immediately into the pool. I got him out and got more towels. Now I had to dry the dog, dry me AND clean up the floors.

"Mama. I'm here. I want to see the Dang Dog again," said Figaro, as she opened the door. Figaro can open doors, cabinets, anything that should remain closed. Miss Mystic darted ahead into the sunroom. Figaro was grumbling and using her ugly words again while sitting in the open doorway. Her eyes never left the poor little dog. I was afraid she was thinking "supper time."

When Figaro told Samson to hide, he scooted under the couch. Samson should have been called Fraidy Cat. He slid under the couch in the sunroom and was now saying, "Oh, NO. You are in here with me! How do I get out? Get away. I have to get away. Get away!" Samson had fur on the bottoms of his feet. He couldn't get traction on anything, but he was mightily trying. You only saw the little black blur of his feet moving; the rest of his fluffy body was still. Finally, he caught traction and off he flew.

Mystic was still in the sunroom but at a cautionary distance. "Can I see? What is it? Will it hurt me? Will it make a big noise?" Curiosity and Mystic's presence gave Samson the courage to come back to the door and watch. Not close enough for contact or even for a little spit to hit him, but he was observing.

"What are you going to do with that thing? It stinks and it acts ugly on the floor," asked Figaro. Her green eyes were narrowed slits. "I do not want it here. It doesn't belong." She looked at the other three cats who were now watching me trying to contain the acrobatic little dog. "Mama, WHICH of these things is NOT like the other?"

The little dog Rascal, Fluffy, Brutus, Caesar, Shakespeare, Bacon, Spot had a collar but no identification. I decided I would try to feed and water him and let him rest a bit before we started trawling the neighborhoods. That meant putting him on the floor. Bupkus, Elroy, Joe, Jonathan, Pesky was not a neutered male. He now decided he had to hump everything in sight. Oh, this was not going over well as he attempted to grab my leg. "NO," I stated firmly. Apparently to Percy, Agamemnon, Zeus, Jupiter, Mars "NO" in Pomeranian means, "Go for it." We had words and I picked up the little beast.

Since the cats had not attacked him and I was tired of trying to hold him, I put him back on the floor. Everything was good. He stayed near me. We went to the kitchen, where he refused to drink or eat. Obviously, if he wouldn't eat, the little critter was traumatized. Who doesn't eat when they have the chance? Again, the cats were close. Gracie looked like Snoopy from Peanuts peering over the counter top. Figaro sat in her regency pose about six feet away. Samson looked from around the bedroom door, and Mystic was trying to get the courage to come out from behind my legs.

I turned my back on little Bozo, Bonkers, Sidney, Adam, Fauntleroy, Kilroy, Killjoy, Mason, Derek and he was gone. I didn't have a clue where he had raced off to. All I could think was, "Please, don't mark your territory, Wendell, David, Marcus, Richard."

"Yip. Yap. Yip! Yap! YIP! YAP!" The cunning little beast, Sleepy, Doc, Dopey, Sneezy, Grumpy, Happy, Bashful, had gone into the land of no return--- my son's bedroom. There was a reason we tried to keep that door closed. James was a collector. He collected many things. As much as he could, he wanted to keep all that stuff in his room. It was not a Man Cave. It is a Cave of Crap. There were taxidermy animals in there. Glass and porcelain elephants and birds. Stuffed animals, junk and enough clothes for a third world country. He couldn't get rid of anything without us having a battle. And now I had lost the dog in the Cave of the Wondrous Collection. "Don't worry, Mama. I'm here. I will find it." Uh-oh. Figaro, who probably outweighed the little dog by fifteen pounds, was sitting at the door to James' room. She was impressively fluffed up. This was a room we say belonged to James, but it really belonged to Figaro. She slept in her special place on her special blanket. The bed and the windows were her lookout point onto the porch and front yard. She knew everyone and everything that occurred from her vantage spot. And here was an intruder.

Figaro had sat down very calmly in front of the door. There was no way that Irving, Joshua, Ohio, Peter was leaving James' room without having to cross her path. I don't think dogs are very bright when it comes to cats. He just kept sitting there yapping at Figaro. At one point, Figaro just yawned and looked up at me. I swear she was smiling so her fangs would glisten in the light. I think I heard her say, "I've got you now, my pretty."

I made my way around her and picked up Walter, Edmund, Ulysses, Fletcher. I was afraid I would have to clean up blood at that point. He started licking and squirming and acting a fool again. I walked toward the door, and Figaro stood and stretched. You know the kind of stretch. She was eighteen feet long by the time she got all the way elongated, and she never stopped looking at the dog. Her paws were spread wide open to reveal her talons, freshly sharpened. Then she raised up and placed her front paws on my leg. I thought, "OH, no. One of us is going to bleed." I leaned over with the dog. She sniffed at him, gave him the evil eye and switched her tail. I am pretty sure Figaro told him, "Any time, any place, Buddy-Boy. I can and will take you."

I decided that I had pushed my luck with the cats, so I cut a length of lightweight rope to use as a leash. We

started off to my backyard neighbors'
house. Little Waldo, Applesauce, Muffin, Adonis wet on
every blade of grass. At this rate, it would be a week from
next Thursday before we got out of the back yard. I
finally got into our neighbor's driveway. My neighbor
didn't claim Rasputin, Vincent, Milan, Sunshine,
Aggravation.

This little dog wanted to be carried everywhere. I
realized that he wasn't used to walking. He kept wanting
me to pick him up. I lifted him up and started down our
drive. I looked back at our house. All four cats were at
the dining room window watching us. They may have
been singing "So long, Farewell, Auf Weidersehen,
Goodbye."

Chuck, Charlie, Snodgrass, Clem and I knocked on
many doors. Only four people opened their doors to
us. No one recognized Tom, Dick, Harry, Pluto, Mickey,
Indiana. I carried the little beastie in the crook of one
arm or the other while he lay on his back and smiled at
me. At one point, I put his back against my chest and
carried him like he was in a baby knapsack. He was
fine. Just as happy as he could be. We both smelled like
wet dog, and it was starting to sprinkle. I didn't think I
could take much more.

Walnut, Pecan, Pine Nuts, Brazil, Poppy and I
returned home. All four cats were waiting. I could hear
the chorus, "Why did you bring that back home? We
don't want it."

Mystic sung a "yeAh, yeAh" when she talked. She
was singing passionately at us as I returned Peanut,
King, Prince to the sunroom. He started looking
around. Samson once again went into hiding. Gracie
leapt to the highest piece of furniture. Without ever
stepping on the floor, she jumped from one thing to
another until she was out of the room.

"YeAH, yeAH, Mama." Bosco, Diablo, Clint, Marvin
had spied her in the room. He was running to
her. "YeAH, I got him. Watch this, Figaro." Mystic
stood on her back feet and looked Percival, McKinley,

Truman, Kennedy in the eye. With a flick so fast that you barely saw the movement, Mystic landed a slap. Figaro was so proud of her sister. I could tell. Figaro got up and walked over to Mystic and touched her on the nose. "Good job, Sissy." Figaro purred.

Winston, Alfred, Whisky, Tango, Foxtrot didn't know what had hit him. He literally rolled over two or three times before he was able to get to his feet. He came running over to claw at my legs until I picked Dufus, Fruit Loop, Nut Job, Einstein up and took him out of the way of the smiling evil sisters.

About this time, thank heaven, Snell and James got home. I had help! Mystic ran to tell them we had an intruder. "YeAH, look what Mama found! It stinks. Do something, Daddy. YeAH, yeAH, Bubba, you don't want it. Make it go away."

Figaro wandered in and looked at them. She returned to the sunroom, leading her daddy and older brother. "Look, Daddy and Bubba. Mama brought THAT into the house." She plopped down and glared.

Since I had canvassed one neighborhood on foot, we decided to take the car and go to the next neighborhood. I would get out and go house to house with Zapata, Jones, Smith, Termite. No one recognized him. Finally, we got to a house where a man came out. His 400-pound dog sat calmly at the door. That man helped a woman who lived across the street with fostering dogs. She came up and agreed to take Mitchel, Ping-Pong, Borneo to her house and to have him checked for a chip the next day.

As soon as we got home, the phone rang. The mama to PONCHO had gotten in from work and was searching the neighborhood. Someone told her I had him, and now Poncho was home where he belonged.

I bathed, then sprayed the house and car with odor killer. The cats continued to walk by and look to see if I were still holding the little mischief maker. I had to break out the catnip and put it in the sunroom where

Poncho had been. "YeAH, yeAH," Mystic said as she rolled into the herbs, getting drunker by the second. Gracie was trying to eat it and was well on her way to being stoned. She remained reposed on the floor and licking the dried herbs from the side of her mouth. Samson lay on his back and looked like he was in heaven. Figaro sat and looked at them and then at me. "You did a bad thing, Mama. I'm watching you." And then she turned and walked out the door.

Gracie's Colorful Language

Well, I have been called every name in the book and then some. My lineage has been questioned back to pre-recorded history. I really don't know where Gracie learned her ugly language, but I feel sure it was from the two cats we lovingly (sort of) call the flying monkeys. After all, Figaro and Mystic were found in a trash dump. They may have associated with some lower-class critters and learned their cussing there.

Our little Gracie is the baby of the feline livestock who live with us. All of them were foundlings. That's a nice way to say feral, thrown away, unloved cats. There is a special place in Hell for those people who toss animals aside or abuse them. Mama called them Sweet Old Boys or Sweet Old Biddies, but that's because Mama didn't cuss. (SOB)

If our son James had his way, we would be running a rescue center for animals. Snell and I are lucky that we have only four cats. James would have brought home every critter known to man. When a muskrat got hit in front of the house, he wanted to bring it back and nurse it to health. Let me set that scene for you. Imagine me in a pale pink linen suit trying to capture this injured muskrat. James is calling his daddy telling him to come help us. Thank goodness, the muskrat ran into the woods. James did tell his daddy that if he saw the muskrat and it was dead to put it in the freezer. He would mount it for posterity. Sigh. You do remember he has studied taxidermy, right?

We have been using Gwinnett Animal Hospital in Snellville for over forty years. Dr. Bill Connolly was our primary physician there until he retired. He forgets that we know where he lives. We have been known to take a dog over to his home for treatment using his kitchen as a medical triage center.

We don't actually have "cats." We have furry babies in our family—all four of them. They should have a personal physician, so we now see Drs. Padgett, Zadspinner or Churchill. We take whoever is available when we can catch a cat. Don't laugh. If you have cats, you know what I am talking about. If you have a dog, you just say, "Come on."

Dr. Katherine Padgett was the vet Gracie and I saw on this particular visit. I love that woman. She was there for us for our little Ramona. That is another story in itself. Ramona inhaled a bot fly larva and was brain-damaged. By the time we had finished treating her, we had bought the University of Georgia a new veterinary wing.

Before we went to the vet, I played classical music for Gracie and spoke soothingly to her. On our way, I prepared her for every turn the car was about to take. The inside of the car was filled with such vicious ugly language that I think blue smoke was coming out of the rear windows.

We arrived at the vet's office and went inside. All the time, Gracie was saying, "NOOOO" in an ear-piercing shriek. When we enter the consultation room, Kat, one of the vet techs, met us there. I had just told Gracie that it would be "Okay," and she had just told me, "NOOOOOOO, ^()*$&%$&%$#$(&, it wouldn't." Kat took Gracie from the carrier and went into the back room. No sound at all. Total silence.

Kat and Dr. Padgett returned with Gracie. They began telling me what a sweetheart she was. How easy it was to trim her nails. I have been trying to give that cat a manicure for three weeks. I get one nail cut, and then someone bleeds and Gracie escapes. "She is such a cutie, just a sweet little thing." Kat continued to sing Gracie's praises.

This demon from Hell is a cute, sweet little thing??? When we are trying to tend to her or trim her nails at home, she is six pounds of venomous rage.

I paid the bill, still in shock that Gracie was being so nice. The moment I opened the door and got outside, her gutter language resumed. The litany of foul expletives escalated as we got closer to the car, and she talked ugly all the way home.

"She is such a cutie, just a sweet little thing," the doctor had said. With me, Gracie was screeching at the top of her lungs. I just knew she was screaming in one long piercing threat, "NOOOOOO, I will get you for this." That sweetness business was all an act. Gracie, the angry voice of Satan, had returned. Linda Blair had nothing on this little cutie. I was considering stopping at the closest church that performed an exorcism.

The moment my husband Snell got the carrier into the kitchen and opened the door, she became silent. She didn't try to come out. She just sat there like a royal personage surveying her lowly servants. Then, she slowly stood, exited the carrier and flicked her tail. She walked straight away from us, tail held high, and with great distaste. I am positive she was saying, "Kiss my fanny, peasants."

Manicures and Pedicures

Do you regularly go for manicures and pedicures? I go every once in a blue moon. I really enjoy them, and I am well behaved in the chair. Occasionally, my son James goes too. He is a little leery of it now, however. Guess the hot wax was what got him on our last visit. Angelica, the nail technician, convinced him to lie back and let her wax his uni-brow. When she did, James levitated a good twelve inches off that chair. He didn't know what had gotten him. Soft voice, warm wax, SNNNAAATTCCCHHH!!! It was an owie.

But as much as I love manicures and pedicures, I hate to give them. And I have to at least once a month. It is not pleasant.

We have four cats plus Mama's little Peppy, who is now at least 172 years old in cat years. Count 'em. Five nails on each of five cats' front paw equals 50 razor-sharp nails. Four nails on each of the back paws equals 40 more. Yes, 90 fingernails, all of which the cats want to keep.

Here is the plan of action: One of us will pick up a cat. I will clip his or her nails, using soothing words of love and encouragement. Then, that cat is put back on the floor and another is picked up. This procedure is repeated until all four of our cats are neatly trimmed.

Here is the truth: Cats can and do communicate warnings to each other.

I secretly close one door to our bathroom. Then James or Snell slowly walks around herding a cat, any cat, toward the bathroom. Cat looks up, sees Snell or James, and makes like a flash of lightning to hide somewhere for days. She telegraphs to the other cats to beware.

Another day goes by, and we see a cat. There is no time to hem one up in the bathroom. One of us leans down, saying nice things to the little puddy-tat. Cat looks up, arches back, and vanishes for another thirty-six hours. All other cats disappear as well.

Two days later, a cat mistakenly lies down and goes to sleep. James swoops in and picks her up! He holds the poor thing in a death grip until we can get to the bathroom. The cat is saying all kinds of dirty words. I have no idea where these cats learned all of their language. It must have been before they came to live with us.

I clip three nails on one paw before the cat gets loose, climbs to the top of James' head, and leaps thirty feet to hit the floor like Mario Andretti cutting a tight curve. The last we see of her is a dark streak and smoke coming up from the cat tread marks on the floor.

Another day passes, and one of the cats wanders into the bathroom. Snell quickly throws his towel over the cat. Snell is naked. I grab the clippers, and Snell flips the encased cat over on its back. Cat informs Snell of what she thinks of his parentage. I manage to cut all of the cat's nails! Success. Snell starts to release cat. Cat leaves skid marks over Snell's chest and back. I doctor Snell's wounds, and all of the other cats disappear.

We continue this prance and dance routine for seven more days. Every time we look at a cat, it disappears. It tells the others and they disappear.

Then, another cat is caught! It is the one who has already had its nails done. Dang it. That cat smirks at us, and I swear I heard it purr, "nanny-nanny-pooh-

pooh," as it marched off with its tail in the air. That little twitch at the tip is a vulgar sign in cat language, I think.

Finally, we get another cat herded into the bathroom, towel thrown, clippers at the ready, and I cut all the nails. We smile at each other. I get out the band aids and campho phenique to deal with our flesh wounds. Do you know that hydrogen peroxide will remove blood stains from fabric, the floor, and the wall?

We are down to one last cat. It is always Samson. Always. He is the big fluffy cat and the only boy in the herd. He is the best hider in the bunch. Samson probably has enough fat stored that he can hibernate during the entire week we are trying to trim nails.

Finally, Samson saunters into a room. Snell, James, and I are on high alert. It has been days since we trimmed anyone's nails. Samson, who isn't the brightest in the bunch, has decided he needs a good combing. Here's my chance to nab him. I have the comb and have started brushing him. His eyes close. Snell gently bends down and slides his hand under Samson's back. All this time I am brushing, singing, and sliding my hand out from under him. This takes at least three or four minutes.

As Snell slowly lifts him, I wrap a towel around his wooly-bear body. We have him. Samson glares death rays at us. He insults all of our parentage and the parentage of everyone we have ever known. As soon as he can, he lunges for the floor. I doctor Snell's slashes as he and I smile at each other. Nine days. It is a record. We trimmed all of the cats' nails in only nine days!!

Only three weeks to go before we start again.

Ramona The Remarkable

Ramona was a little fluffy black and white kitten that Mama and I brought home one New Year's Day. We had gone over to Margie and John Sawyer's house to feed their inside cats and the outside strays while they were away. As I came out of the house, I just reached down and scooped this little fur ball into my arms and handed her to Mama who held her all the way home. When we went into the house, our other cat, Miss Molly, walked up and looked at us. "What in the name of heaven are you doing with that thing? Don't expect me to raise it. I have enough to do with the rest of you." Eventually, Molly and Ramona became close and loved one another, but trust me, their burying the claws wasn't overnight, and wasn't always pleasant.

Ramona was a cuddly cat. She liked to ride wrapped around my neck and would lie on my shoulder while I read and watched television. Miss Molly, also a foundling, wanted to sit in someone's lap and be the sole proprietor. There were a few struggles until everyone learned to trust everyone else—most of the time.

At that time, our cats were allowed to go outside and come back into the house. They knew the call to come home. Three claps and a call of their names followed by three more claps. They never seemed to go very far because when we called, they would be at the door within a few minutes.

LIFE IS HARD SOFTEN IT WITH LAUGHTER

We have a couple of old barns on our property. We didn't know it at the time, but a rabbit had birthed some babies in one of the old buildings. Ramona brought us one. It wasn't hurt. She was just bringing us a present. She was upset when we took it back to the barn and turned it loose. You could see it in her eyes, "Daddy, WHY? I brought you a present." We bragged on her and gave her lots of attention for being a good hunter but asked her not to bring another bunny home.

One morning Ramona was sneezing like crazy. We wondered what in the world she had gotten into to cause the sneezing fits. Later that week, we found out. Bot flies are an evil beast that have migrated here from South America. The fly lays an egg on the skin or fur of an animal. The egg hatches into a cuterebra (larva/worm) and burrows into the flesh to live until it matures. Cats seem to be the only animals that inhale the egg. It matures in the sinuses, and once it enters the larval stage it begins to eat its way through the sinus cavity into the brain. Ramona was a victim.

That morning Ramona suddenly screamed and fell onto her side. We went to the vet who wasn't sure what was happening. Ramona couldn't walk because she continuously fell over on her side. When she tried to walk, she tottered in a tight little circle and then fell over. She cried and whimpered in pain almost continuously. The vet sent us to University of Georgia Veterinary School for treatment. Ramona's x-rays, CT scans, MRIs and all other evaluations are used now to train other veterinary students about bot flies. Yes, I agree, one wing of the UGA Vet School should be named for Ramona. I'm pretty sure we paid for it.

After weeks of living at the hospital, we brought Ramona home. She had to have special treatment. Snell and I got up every four hours and fed Ramona through a feeding tube in her neck. It took one hour to prepare, feed, and clean up. We repeated this ritual twenty-four hours a day for eight weeks before she made enough progress to have the feeding tube removed. We taught her to drink by giving her mini-moos of half and half creamer in water. I touched my finger tip to the milk and then to her mouth. She finally began to "taste," and then I could lead her to the saucer and feed her milky water one drop at a time. We did whatever was necessary, and we would do it all over again. When she ate a third of a shrimp, I called the vet school and the Head of the Neurology Department did a happy dance. Really, I have the video.

Eventually, Ramona was able to feed herself and could find her water. We still watched her carefully because we didn't want her to dehydrate. She unsteadily walked in circles and wanted to be carried and held more often. I am afraid this story ends sadly. She was doing so well we started letting her walk around more by herself. We became careless about closing off areas of the house. It didn't appear that she could climb or jump, but one night she got on the side of the indoor therapy pool that we had installed for me and fell into it. I still can't go into the pool without crying.

Ramona's troubles and treatment were on going through my mother's illness and my cancer. Ramona was the distraction to take my mind off all the illness that seemed to be consuming my life. Every little bit of progress she made was like a momentous milestone towards normalcy. Her death, which could have been avoided if we had just kept the doors closed, represents one of the saddest times in our lives.

Health

Technicolor Ta=Ta's. It ain't purdy

Squished is a Necessary Evil

I have all of my medical tests performed the same month each year, including my mammogram. The month of October is the time that ghouls and whoo-doodies come alive and get mischievous. I tend of think of the Big Squishier as a Halloween Goblin. The huge presser foot is one of the nastiest villains I have to face each year. I am not tiny. Jewel, the technician, always brings out the BIG cookie sheets for me. She keeps them fresh in the freezer. I believe the reasoning is to ensure I will be boldly awake when the machine exerts 1,125 pounds of pressure per square inch to flatten my boobie. I have a lot of ta-ta space. I also bruise easily. Think about it. Technicolor ta-tas. Trust me. They ain't purdy.

What should have been a routine mammogram turned out to be a bit more of an adventure. Not all adventures are fun, but they are learning experiences. I learned how to cuss in college. I learned from the best, a bunch of Navy SEALs. I can smile while I do it, too. It is frightening.

As I said, I am well endowed. I am not happy about it, but I've got 'em. Ladies who don't 'have 'em want 'em. Walk a mile in my brassiere and see if you still feel that way.

LIFE IS HARD SOFTEN IT WITH LAUGHTER

One of my friends refers to mammograms as being pancaked. Women come in all sizes. She said she can go in and the technician can hold a flashlight on one side and read her breast tissue from the other. That is small. To me having a mammogram is like taking a rolling pin and trying to flatten a sixteen-pound bowling ball into a 12 x 14-inch cookie sheet. When I come in, the technician gets the plates out, ices 'em up, and attempts to squash living tissue to death.

I have been going to Eastside Diagnostic Center in Snellville for years. I know only Jewel by name because she is the technician who has done my pancaking for most of my visits. She runs the Iron Maiden. Jewel truly tries to make what could be an embarrassing and uncomfortable situation quick and easy. She is a kind, gentle woman with a most pleasant personality. She has the job from hell and no warm blood coursing through her body. No matter what she does, she has cold hands.

Let me tell you a little about the procedure. Some of you may not have had the joy of experiencing this modern medical phenomenon. First, the temperatures of the rooms are at 65 degrees Fahrenheit or lower. They say it is so that germs can't survive. It also shuts down the chances of air borne diseases. Yeah. I hear that. It also shuts down the patient's circulatory system to all outer extremities. It is as cold as a witch's ta-ta in a snowstorm.

There you stand. Naked as a jaybird on your top half, while your ta-tas are being pulled and pushed into unnatural positions. Jewel smiles kindly as she begins to lower the press. "You are going to feel a little pressure." She lowers the press some more. "You are doing great, just a little more pressure." She tightens the vice grips even more. "Just one more turn." By this time, you think "If you don't get this done, I am going to reach over with my free hand and snatch you bald headed."

"One more little turn."

This hurts. It really hurts.

Then Jewel says "Hold your breath while I take the picture. Hold your breath. Hold, hold," I got news for you, lady, after the third turn on this Iron Maiden, I couldn't catch my breath. I've got no air in me to hold. Just shut up and take the picture.

Then she repeats the same torture on the other side.

Sometimes, for fun, she decides the first series of scans were not good enough, and, how exciting, we get to repeat the process. Yep. Just love this day.

Well, I got THE CALL. Not the letter you get within seven days of the procedure. I did get that, but I got THE CALL first. I appreciated Dr. Peter Mann's office calling and telling me to come in for my annual pelvic review. Another delightful experience for women. "Excuse me, sir. I know we have never met when I was fully clothed but let me shake your hand before you delve into the shadows of darkness, going where no man should ever have to go. Hey, I had a baby. I had Snell fixed. I don't use that thing anymore!"

Back to THE CALL from Peter Mann's nurse at Gwinnett Gynecology. "Dr. Mann received the results of your recent mammogram and would like for to have it repeated, blah, blah, blah, will magnify, blah, blah, blaaaah, calcium deposits, blah, blah, blah-d-blah-blah." You know I only heard "repeat the test," and my brain atrophied, and my breasts began to throb.

As I said, I do all my annual testing in the same month. So, after I got the call, I saw my general physician. He asked when I had last had my mammogram, and I told him the date and that I was scheduled for another to magnify and "area of concern." Don't you just love it? "An area of concern" when they mean "You got a spot of something that looks really scary, so we want to pinch the devil out of you again to be sure that we can see that sucker really well."

My GP made a huge mistake. I still had blue and green ta-tas from the first procedure, and I had just gotten the call to repeat the joyful activity. I am sure he was trying to alleviate any concerns and fears on my part. "Oh, it's nothing. People have calcium deposits, and stuff that are just nothing." Instead of making me feel better, he made me feel diminished. As if my concerns were my imagination, and I was silly to even give a second thought about any of the possibilities. I wasn't weeping and wailing. I certainly wasn't begging for a pitcher of ice water and a "poor, poor baby." Just an acknowledgement that it was okay for me to be a little uneasy about the need to repeat the mammogram. He should have tried to reassure me that I was in good medical hands.

I am not a person who overreacts. I don't panic. I can butterfly a wound so prettily it would make an ER doctor weep from the sheer beauty of it. I have been a teacher. Vomit doesn't bother me. Blood doesn't bother me. I have been in autopsies. Stench doesn't bother me. I have been given devastating news. I have had to deliver life-changing, gut wrenching messages, I have held people as they receive the most horrible news imaginable, so don't pooh-pooh and don't diminish me with "Oh, it isn't a big deal." It is a big deal for me. How about a response that is more comforting and acknowledges my trepidation. "I know that causes you concern. I am glad you are having this looked into. You have a great doctor. I believe you will be okay. Call my office if you need us."

So, I went back to another fun-filled day of breast compression. Nurse Margie was the technician on cruelty duty that day. She was just delightful. We laughed and cut up as if we had known each other forever. As she wedged me into to the Iron Maiden, Margie, like Jewel, made an uncomfortable situation as pleasant as possible. She explained what had been identified as a suspicious place and showed me the first set of films. She called it "Your little star cluster." Afterwards, she showed me the second, more magnifying set of pictures. She identified the spot that had caught the doctor's eye and showed me another area that looked similar, but was in fact, a previously identified calcium deposit.

It is a good thing that I can walk down 78 highway buck-naked and not care anymore, because I had to sit in an unattractive, open gown, always too small, in the dressing area for what seemed like eons of time. I got to visit with many other half-naked women who came and went. Finally, the doctor finished reading the films. Margie came back to the room and told me I could dress. Great, maybe it is all okay and I can go home with my little star cluster. Instead of leading me to the escape door, Margie took me deeper into the bowels of hell to meet Dr. Biafore. She was one of the most beautiful women I have ever seen. She smiled and made one as comfortable as one can in a cold room while looking at your ta-tas on a light box.

It was comforting that I would be leaving the center knowing what was seen and what would be done. She explained that I needed a biopsy. The film revealed what could be calcifications but could be something else. I had a number of calcifications, and there was a strong possibility that this was another. However, this place was new and in a location different from previous mammograms. Tissue samples would be needed.

Now. I was thinking I had to be held captive again in the Iron Maiden and have Dr. Biafore use a drill press and bit for a tissue sample. All I could think was Dr. GP, who made me feel small about my concerns. I envisioned The Iron Maiden with his left testicle. I could hear the sinister tone in my voice as I smiled and advised him, "You will feel a little pressure."

The Biopsy

I left my tale with you just as I was about to have a breast biopsy. My routine mammogram had shown a "suspicious" spot.

Why are all the hospital gowns missing at least one tie, and it is always the one in the most strategic place? And why in the world can you see your breath in the waiting room? Can't we at least have a little heat? We may not have our dignity, but at least some warmth would help. I mean I was about to have a ¾ inch hole drilled into my frozen breast. Can't we thaw it out a little bit?

Eventually, I was led down a long hallway. It made me think of the movie "The Green Mile," but this one was in shades of purples and greys. I think the intercom was playing "Onward Christian Soldiers".

I was left in a room with an angry, hungry looking machine and a large pink chair. I was told to sit in the chair and lean forward. When you are short and have big boobs, leaning forward is sort of a persistent state. The nice nurse with the cold hands pressed my left breast onto an icy plate and then dropped an anvil on it. I was clenched in the vice-grip jaws of the instrument of torture.

Trust me, if anyone yelled "Fire!" I was going to be toast. There was no escaping these jaws of this drilling machine. Rescuers would find me dangling there by one boob with my little feet running in place.

The drill press, I was sure it has a very impressive name, with a rectangular hole in the top presser plate was waiting for me. The very beautiful and soft-spoken Dr. Biafore explained the hole was so the "area of concern" could be reached by the doctor. The entire time you are pinched in place, two nurses are setting up equipment and swabbing your "area of concern" with ugly orange betadine solution. Please note: We were still saying "area of concern," not scary, malicious, evil spot that was growing by leaps and bounds. The word cancer has not been used.

Demonetta, one of the nurses, smiled and told me that I was in "proper placement." Suddenly, people started coming at me with LONG needles. "You will feel a little prick as we numb your breast." Little prick, my Aunt Fannie! And Uncle Herman, too!

I wish I could remember the two nurses' names, but Demonetta and Beelzebubbette, her cohort in nursing care, were the only names that I can remember. They were compassionate, gentle, funny and clearly trying to make me comfortable. They explained everything to me, except the part about the drinking straw sized needle hurting like hell as it forced its way under extreme pressure into my frozen ninny. But they tried, telling me what the equipment was and how the doctor would proceed with taking a small sample and then a film, another sample, another film, etc. That 14-inch syringe deleted all the fight or flight adrenaline from me. I was trapped and couldn't escape.

Dr. Biafore left the room and returned carrying something. Personally, I thought she took her own sweet time getting herself in there. It was probably all of two minutes I had to wait, but I was trapped in the c-clap of death, and she was strolling in with a smile on her face. She was a lovely lady with a delightful personality, and someday I will be able to have nice thoughts of her again. She was carrying a rectangular blue box about two inches wide and six inches long with a long needle attached to one end. Beelzebubbette was talking to me about growing up in the Atlanta area and trying to get me to look at her. I ain't no dummy. I knew she was trying to distract me, and she knew it wasn't working.

Then I heard this popping sound. Dr. Biafore had attached the drill bit to the drill press while Beelzebubbette was talking to me. Suddenly, I heard a different pitched popping sound. That popping sound was her sinking a well in my left breast. This procedure continued for at least three days or perhaps three minutes.

When Dr. Biafore stopped to study the screen showing the drill bit placement, she held her hands in a prayer position. Was this habit? Was she sending up prayers that the sink hole in her victim was properly placed? Maybe she held her gloved hands that way to protect them touching anything, but it looked like she was praying. I knew I was praying. And with what appeared to be an oil rig erected around me, I couldn't get my hands in proper prayer position, but trust me, I was praying my hardest.

Dr. Biafore smiled and said, "good news. We have reached the area of concern." She sank a clip of metal into the area of concern. That little piece of metal would be left in the spot where the tissue was excised so further tests would show where the biopsy was performed. I was hoping this clip would be large enough that I could wear a magnetic name badge, and it would perform a breast lift.

I know you have heard of the old saying about "good news/bad news." Well, the findings were sort of the "bad news is bad enough, but it could be a whole lot worse" news.

Bedside Manner

You have heard of the old bad news/good news shtick. Well, this was "the bad news is bad enough, but it could be a whole lot worse" news. I had cancer, and I didn't want it. I did not ask for it. I did not plan on keeping it and I was certainly not inviting it back if I survived it.

I met with my gynecologist, Dr. Peter Mann, for my annual, fun-filled afternoon and results from the breast biopsy. Dr. Mann has received many awards. He should get one for "Best Bedside Manner." Also, he should get an award for best examination rooms. Patients have a TV, a heater, and cute little stirrup covers so your feet aren't on cold, hard metal. Nice, isn't it? Buck-naked as the day you were born, but you are warm and comfortable as possible.

There I was sitting on this hard, narrow little cot, wearing a paper shirt that is at least six inches from closing in the front and a paper sheet. He took my hand and told me how pleased he was to see me again.

Now, I was thinking, I am naked, wearing a totally un-accessorized paper vest, and you act like "Let's have a hot fudge sundae and chat." I liked it. He made me as comfortable as possible considering my lack of wardrobe, and he was about to make like the Nautilus and go deep diving.

Dr. Mann sat down and told me that he had the biopsy results, which showed I had Ductal Carcinoma in Situ, DCIS for short. I think, four years of Latin, I can translate that into cancer in a milk duct, in place, contained. My brain short circuited. Carcinoma was all I heard. Carcinoma meant cancer. Yep, total brain shut down. Well, off we go on another adventure.

This kind and gentle doctor also told me to stop all hormones. Do you know what that means? I do. When I told Snell, he got a wild-eyed frightened look. We have been through hot flashes before. My internal combustion engine was about to be kicked into high gear. Snell and James had best get out their cold weather woolies because I will burst into flames at a moment's notice. It isn't a pretty sight, and you might need a layer of asbestos to handle the ignition.

Dr. Mann explained where the DCIS was located, what it was, and what the next steps should be. He assured me that a lumpectomy followed with medication and perhaps radiation was all that would be needed. I was confident that I could handle this diagnosis and treatment as soon as my brain began to function again. Dr. Mann provided me with several names of surgeons to discuss treatment.

I begin calling surgeons and scheduling appointments. The first surgeon I could get an appointment with was a woman. I had heard good things about her from others. I thought she would be a good choice. She came in and said, "I am Dr. XYZ. You have breast cancer. Do you want a lumpectomy or a mastectomy? You need to let the office know by this Friday." Then, she left. "Hey! You may be having a bad day, but you just made mine a whole lot worse." I thought to myself. Fired her before she got all the way through the doorway.

I was thinking she spent less than three minutes with me, and I hated her guts. Wow! First impressions:

Bad Bedside Manner. I was visualizing her, and my GP being trapped in the Iron Maiden for a couple of hours. His left testicle and her right breast with just a little more pressure applied at regular intervals should change their attitudes. Sweet Old Boy meet Sweet Old Biddy, as my mama would graciously call them.

My quest for the perfect surgeon continued. My breasts are fondled by several more people. Mostly doctors. Finally, my appointment with the surgeon I had first thought would be my best choice arrived. Yes, I was right. I saw the other doctors, but Dr. Victor Pavamani was the man for me. If you ever have the opportunity to meet Dr. Pavamani, you will like him. He was my daddy's surgeon and was wonderful to Mama, too.

When Mama had to have a hysterectomy, she had to stay overnight in the hospital. I came into the hospital early and ran into Dr. Mann, her doctor, as well, in the hallway. He was telling me how well Mama was doing. When we entered Mama's hospital room, we found her and Dr. Pavamani lying in the bed together, holding hands. That was just the kind of man he was. He saw her name on the roster and went to see her. He had her smiling and laughing. Good bedside manner, caring, interested in his patients, and funny.

On Wednesday morning, I showed up at Eastside Diagnostic Center where Dr. Biafore and her trusty cold-handed, warm-hearted nurses again tightened me into the c-claps of the Iron Maiden and plunge a needle the size of a Varsity drinking straw into my breast. She injected blue dye and then inserted a long thin wire as a marker for Dr. Pavamani. This wire was the antennae he would use to find his way into the center of the cancer site.

Oh Joy! Remember as little kids how much fun it was to play with crutches and ride in wheelchairs. It wasn't as much fun the morning of my procedure. I got to ride in a wheelchair across the breeze way to the hospital. It was just that-- a breezeway where you felt the open air on every exposed area. It was not enclosed, and it was breezy. And I was wearing nothing but a sheet and an antenna.

Picture this, I was sitting in a wheelchair with a wire thrust into my left breast. I was being told to not move the wire and to be very still. I was sure the wire was broadcasting a signal to a satellite somewhere that says "Warning. Warning. This is not a test."

The office secretary pushed me outside under the covered walk to the hospital entrance some distance away. Open to the world, the breezeway was windy as all get out. I was trying to hold on to my sheet, not move the wire, and not cuss out loud. I had visions of leeches and bloodletting whirring through my mind.

I was rolled into Room 12 to await my fate and Dr. Pavamani. I had a very pleasant time in this room. Ms. Jane Alexander, the Queen Mum of Gwinnett County Education and the Eastside H2U volunteers (those people in the coral jackets), came by to visit. Ms. Jane was volunteering at the hospital but came over to the surgery center to see me. She was there in her pretty hat and genuinely lovely smile. We visited and laughed about her second great-grandchild who was born the day before and who was known to one and all as BOO because he was due at Halloween.

My husband Snell met four or five people he knew in the surgery center. After living in Snellville all of his life and teaching/counseling at South Gwinnett High School for thirty-four years, he frequently meets people he knows. Actually, he is either related to them or to their parents or through school. So, more people came into the room to say hello and give kind wishes. Think about this. I was lying there under a thin sheet, naked and with a wire sticking straight up and making a point above my left ta-ta. With no make-up, I greatly resembled a possum in the throes of a panic attack. I was smiling at many total strangers and anxiously awaiting the nurse with the kick-a-poo joy juice.

Dr. Pavamani made his way through the throngs of visitors to reassure me that all would go well and not to worry. He was laughing and cutting up with the staff and people he knew who are now in the room. The nurses who did my pre-op stopped by to say hello.

The anesthesiologist and his assistant came by to tell bad jokes. Everyone was having a great time, everyone except me. Then entered Nurse Tammy, and she had the good stuff. Now, I was having a great time.

At this point in my life, I had a 93-year-old mother who couldn't see well and refused to acknowledge that she couldn't hear. A husband who doesn't hear, a special needs child who doesn't listen, a traumatically brain injured cat, and two kittens that masquerade as flying monkeys. So, what's cancer......?

Hormones v/s Horrormones

Please hum Carmen Miranda's "I'm having a heat wave, a tropical heat wave" as you read this.

And the saga continues. Are you as tired of this breast cancer story as I am? Well, here is another part. But in this one, I get to glow—literally.
When I was working at Parkview High School, I was going through menopause, and hot flashes were a very common part of my day. I think "The Change" took ten years to complete. "The Change" was not a change. It was an encounter with purgatory four or five times a day.

Two of my co-workers would break into choruses of "Tropical Heat Wave" as I hastily went through the office door praying for a snow storm. I would have torn off all my clothes if I could have gotten away with it. But I worked in a high school and it wasn't good to scare the adolescents. Although, the sight of me naked might have reduced the number of sexual encounters between the kids. All of them were walking hormones.

I worked with Ed Hunt. He was the most marvelous Assistant Principal in the world. Kids often told me that he was the only AP who could make you feel good about being punished. He was an amazingly positive man with a great manner with kids and one my favorite people in the world. Ed liked to use my office for conferences. It was located in the center part of the school and had comfortable chairs. His office was located in one the farthest buildings on campus, but trouble always happened nearer my section of the school than his. I frequently sat in on the disciplinary conferences, too.

When Ed needed to use my office for a student disciplinary issue, he would knock and almost simultaneous unlock the door. At the time, I had an industrial strength fan. It blew on low, medium, and cyclone. This particular day was one spent in the infernos of hell. I had locked the door, turned the fan to cyclone, and removed my sweater. I admit a pullover sweater was a stupid idea. I should have been in a halter top. I was standing in front of the fan, contemplating filling the cups of my bra with ice, when I heard a knock on the door and the turning of the key. I threw myself against the door, yelling, "Just a minute, Ed!" I barely got my sweater back on when I pulled the door open. There stood Ed with two or three "rounders" who were in trouble. I sat in on the conference, hoping I was not sweating too badly. When they left, I realized I was wearing my sweater inside out.

Let's fast forward to where I am at the part of my cancer treatment that involved not taking my hormones. Yep, are you beginning to hear the faint melody of Carmen's song. I was off all hormones and taking Evista, which is a prescription hormone blocker. Ductal Carcinoma is an estrogen-fed cancer. In order to starve the cancer, you must cut off its food supply. That was what the doctors told me. It meant going through menopause for the second time. Like the first time wasn't bad enough, Evista caused me to burst into flames fifty-five minutes after I swallowed that pill. I thought I was burning the cancer cells from the inside out. Everyone knew I would cut their hands off if they touched the thermostat. I didn't care if it is winter, leave the air conditioner on and overlook the light dusting of snow covering the floors.

I really should dedicate this essay to Ed Hunt, Snell, James, and to all those men who were wise enough to keep the freezer stocked with ice cream, their winter jackets nearby, and their mouths shut.

I was trying to keep the air conditioning at a reasonable temperature. I think forty-five degrees is reasonable, don't you? My boys complained that it was warmer outside in December than it was in the house. Snell would come in and immediately begin putting on flannel shirts and heavy socks. I frequently had to change my night clothes, wringing them out and hanging them to dry. Snell encouraged the cats to sleep next to him because they gave off body heat. James stayed upstairs almost all of the time. He had his winter comforter and a blanket on his bed. He also had a heating pad and a cat that slept next to him. James slept in long sleeved flannel pajamas, but no one said a word of complaint. I could blast furnace their eyebrows off with a sigh.

Have you ever heard of a woman in love having a certain glow? Well, when you are without hormones and going through menopause/cancer treatment/hell you don't glow. You turn beat red, sweat like a pig in heat, and snarl at anyone who gets within five feet of your space. I'll tell you what glow is. When you have immediate internal combustion, you make like a beacon. Men feel warm in your presence, not because of love or lust, but because you have a core temperature of 126 degrees. Ice cubes melt three feet away from "the glow".

Menopause—a pause in the men in your life if they are smart. They leave you alone and set the thermostat at fifty-five degrees. The meanest of men and the most ferocious of animals will cower in fear that at any minute your head will blow off and you will spew vicious statements and threats at them. You are dripping wet with hot, steamy sweat, and you have a headache, but for what? For having ovaries. It isn't right, people. It isn't fair. No man in his right mind would ever say they share the pain, that they empathize with you. They just stay as far away from you as possible and nod yes to anything you growl. I have a pair of cattle emasculators from my grandparents' farm. They hang in our barn. If you have a man who is pooh-poohing your inner industrial furnace, call me. I will lend them to you.

Modesty Not on Your Life

odesty would be a word I would not associate with cancer. I've established my lack of need for it through this experience. I believed the world had seen all I've got. There was nothing left to hide. I can't count how many people have handled my left ta-ta, and now that Dr. Pavamani had finished carving on it, I had to find a new "handler".

In 2005, Mama had gallbladder surgery and a cancerous tumor was found inside. Dr. Satvir Singh was her oncologist. Mama called him her "Handsome Prince." Dr. Singh wore a turban. The first time she met him, she was in a morphine induced haze. Mama woke up and saw her handsome prince talking to her and holding her hand.

That man was wonderful, a real prince, to her. She could not see well. He would hold her hand and walk her down the hallways. They genuinely liked one another. Whenever they met they would love on each other. As Mama would leave, he would hug her. Mama would say "I love you." In response, he would laugh, kiss her on the top of her head, and say, "I love you, too."

When I had to choose an oncologist for my cancer treatment, I went straight for Mama's handsome prince charming. On the day that Dr. Singh walked into his exam room and found me waiting, he stopped short and pointed at me with a questioning look in his eye. I nodded my head. He shook his and said, "I'm so sorry."

159

During my visits to him, Dr. Singh always asked about Mama. He always sent his love and best wishes. When she was hospitalized shortly before her death, he would stop by and visit with her. He even called the house to ask about her when she came home for hospice care. Mama died a few days before the end of my radiation treatments. When I told him she had passed away, he stood in the office lobby and held me. We cried together for the longest time. What a special man.

Snell, Dr. Singh, and I discussed my DCIS and the treatment options. He recommended radiation. All the medical people I had seen told me that if I had to have cancer mine was the best kind to have. Dr. Singh told me the recovery rate for it was extremely high. My surgeon, Dr. Pavamani, had gotten clear margins, and the lymph nodes were healthy. He said Dr. Pavamani had essentially left me cancer free, but I needed treatment to stay that way. DCIS is a slow growing cancer. Fortunately, mine had been found early.

Dr. Singh made me feel so much better. I had been scared out of my wits, and I really didn't have many wits left. He said this was an early warning to slow down and take better care of myself.

Dr. Singh referred me to Dr. John Gargus at the Radiotherapy Center of Georgia for the radiation therapy I needed. The two men conferred and planned a strategy for my treatments. Dr. Gargus looked just like my pediatrician, Dr. Perry, whom I last saw when I was probably thirteen years old. I don't know why the correlation was comforting, but it was. He even sounded like Dr. Perry, soft and soothing.

The Radiotherapy Center of Georgia was one of the prettiest buildings I had ever seen. It was a calming place. There was a tree in the center of treatment areas in back that was decorated for every holiday. The staff were so kind and delightful. The positive atmosphere made the whole experience less frightening.

LIFE IS HARD SOFTEN IT WITH LAUGHTER

By this time in my journey, I was so accustomed to people wanting to look and feel of my breasts that I automatically assumed the position. As I mentioned earlier, cancer and modesty do not work well together. You know how you are uncomfortable meeting a new person in a gown that covers less than one breast? Well, guess what. Dr. Gargus has BIG gowns. They are fabric and warm.

Assume the Position

At the radiology center, I met with my doctor to go over my treatment plan which has been designed by the medical team of my oncology and radiology doctors. At this point, Dr. Gargus and his staff became my primary contact. Dr. Singh, my oncologist, would receive reports, but I would not go back to see him until treatment was almost complete. I think because of the personality of Dr. Singh and his genuine like of my mother, Dr. Singh stayed in touch a little more than most oncologists would have.

After my interview and explanation of treatments, I was introduced to the technicians, Marina and Carmen, AKA the Beast Masters. These two women would soon become my BFFs (Breast Friends Forever).

To prepare me for my series of retreatments, I had to have a body mold created. Marina helped me down on a bean bag sack. Well, from my perspective, it felt like that. As she pushed and pulled to shape me and the bag together, it began to harden and take on the contour of my body, including all my back-fat rolls.

Marina did a series of CT scans, marking and measuring tiny fractions of space and finally drawing all the points for radiation treatment on my skin and the bean bag. Once she had the bag formed, I had to lie still in that contortionist's position for another thirty or forty minutes until the bean bag hardened. Now I could be permanently posed in that position. It would be uncomfortable because of the location of the DCIS, my left arm had to pretzeled into an awkward position, and my back and shoulders were twisted.

This hardened form would be placed on the table for each treatment. I assume the position for the length of each radiation exposure. Carmen would assist with properly positioning me into the mold. Those markers on the mold line up with indicators the machine would read. My body, the mold, and the machine had to be perfectly aligned each time.

All I can say is that if I had been hung from the ceiling, I would have looked more like a Marc Chagall Mobile than a human being. I had blue lines covering my upper torso. My breast was now more greenish – yellow from the lumpectomy, and the blue streaks stood out very prettily.

Fried Chicken Skin

Before I tell you anymore, I want to give you some tips on treatments and consultations. Always bring someone with you to listen to what is being said. Beforehand, write your questions down and give your partner a copy. You will not remember everything you are told, and you won't ask all your questions. Your brain is still in a state of shock and denial. The information is just too much to absorb at one time.

I made the mistake of leaving Snell in the waiting room. He wears two hearing aids and can't hear thunder. But in a quiet room, he usually gets all of the conversation. He did great with all the doctors. He filled in things and asked those questions that I forgot. I didn't ask him to come back in the room with the radiation specialist. I don't know why, the thought just didn't occur to me that I would need him, but I did. I always do.

I was given the initial overview of what to expect during the radiation therapy. During treatments, I asked the Radiation Specialist things that I know she had told me in our first meeting. She always explained everything thoroughly and never became put out with me, or if she did, she hid her frustrations well.

And this is very important: no question is too dumb. You don't know all this stuff. You don't talk in this language. Ask your question and ask it again if you don't understand the response. The medical staff would rather spend the time making you aware and comfortable with your treatment plan than have you up-tight, fearful, and confused.

Stop worrying about how you look. There is always someone who looks a lot worse than you do. Keep things in perspective. You are taking positive action and taking charge of yourself. Who cares if you don't have hair or eyebrows? You are doing something to help yourself. Without make-up, I look like a bleached-out possum. Trust me, you will see worse. The medical staff and other patients won't care, and neither should you.

If something hurts or doesn't feel right, speak up. You may not have been placed into your body mold just right. Maybe you are coming down with a cold. Tell the Beast Masters so they can be aware and prepared. Unless you tell them, they don't know what you need.

If something is going on in your life that is traumatic, tell them. They need to know. I was exhausted from taking care of our little Ramona, the brain injured cat. My mama was in the hospital and not doing well. I was holding on by my fingernails, and they were breaking off rapidly. One day while I was laying on the table under the radiation beast, I began to cry. I had received a call that morning that Ron, one of my dearest friends with whom I talked on the phone or through email every day, had died suddenly early that day. I was having trouble lying there for fifteen or twenty minutes absolutely still with nothing but my brain actively moving through various stages of exhaustion and grief. The staff needed to know what was happening in my life. I told them, and they allowed for those moments.

When I first met Marina, she gave me a list of suggestions. It was recommended that you use 100% Aloe Vera Gel on your treatment area after every therapy session and several more times during the day, especially after bathing. It soothed the "burn." And yes, you do have fried chicken skin. It will discolor. The texture will be odd, but you should expect that. Eventually, it will go back to normal—sort of. My ta-ta was white, almost all the color was bleached out.

You cannot use just any deodorant. Arm and Hammer Essentials was the one I chose from the list. It did not have anything in it to cause problems. Many deodorants have aluminum oxides and other chemicals than can cause burns and irritation to very tender skin. Some of the chemicals in bath powders and deodorants can cause errors to occur in radiation treatment, too.

Ladies, you can't shave the area of treatment. For breast cancer patients, that is your underarms. You can shave the one not being blasted by radioactive waves. My suggestion is do not wear sleeveless anything. Just don't.

Buy a big box of corn starch and use it liberally. It is like placing a thin layer of silk between your tender skin and your clothing. It really does keep fabrics from rubbing against you. It is cooling and has nothing in it to cause you a problem. Corn starch is heavier than talcum powder, which flies all over the place and doesn't give you that silky protection against friction and fabrics.

Several women were having breast cancer treatment at the same time I was. Except for the double mastectomy woman, we all wore bras. Yes, we talked about these things in the waiting room and dressing areas. We talked about a lot of things, but "over the shoulder boulder holders" is the topic of this part of the story. I found that I was actually much more comfortable with a bra. Because my surgery involved lymph glands and breast/nipple areas, I found a soft, smooth cupped bra was my breast friend. It didn't give me the support I liked from my Flying Buttress style underwire, but it did help me to be more comfortable. Several others in treatment at the same time told me that they wore bras that were similar. The woman who had a double mastectomy wore a silk scarf tied like a halter top so that her recovering surgical site was a little more protected from her clothing

LIFE IS HARD SOFTEN IT WITH LAUGHTER

All of us in the morning group talked about what was happening with us. We all agreed that keeping the aloe vera gel warm was essential. We decided that the dressing area should have a bottle warmer equipped with a jug of aloe vera gel. Those dressing areas were not just cold, they were damned cold, and if you hadn't kept your aloe vera with you, it was like rubbing an ice cube on singed flesh.

Only use a gentle soap for sensitive skin. I bought Kroger's brand of unscented, sensitive skin, liquid soap. A couple of the ladies said they used Dove for sensitive skin. You want to avoid any product that has an irritant in it. Some fragrances can be a problem. Do not use hot water; comfortably warm is what you will find is best. Think of yourself as intensely sunburned. Fried chicken breast without the batter is the best description I can give you.

A person having radiation treatment is basically healing for months, long after the last treatment. Your treatment and the healing process come from the inside out. Cut yourself some slack. Eat a Hershey bar. Cry a little. Hell, cry a lot. It is okay to be scared. You can't be fearless all of the time. Life is hard. Soften it with a little laughter and a lot of chocolate.

The Dreaded Three Headed Hydra

The radiology technicians, Marina and Carmen, better known as the Glow Girls, are the keepers of the three-headed hydra. Do you remember from your high school biology class learning to use the microscope for the first time? The teacher put a single drop of water on the slide, and you could see the hydra with all of its arms. If you don't remember, think about the 1960's Hercules movies, such as *The Seven Perils of Hercules*. That big critter with all the heads was a Hydra, and Hercules had to defeat it. He would cut off one head and another would regenerate. Any of you remember Medusa? Same principle. For you younger folks, refer to the Power Rangers on TV and one of their many multi-headed beasties.

This machine looks like a hydra to me. It has three differently shaped heads. Marina or Carmen places me in my personally shaped body bag, which is now hard and cold. I lay on my back, with my left arm twisted at an odd angle. Looking up into the faces of the three heads, I wonder what each has in store for me. The heads move over and around the table on which I am stretched. When the Glow Girls get me in proper placement, they exit the room to a control center that makes the Command Star Ship Enterprise pale in comparison.

Treatment sessions vary. The longest session is a little over thirty minutes. Those longer periods are during the first therapy sessions. During the first treatment, Marina and Carmen keep double checking measurements and drawing on me again.

On the first day, the Glow Girls trap you, the victim, in just the right position and make sure all the marks are perfect. Nurse Rutledge, Hydra Herder, comes in to take over the procedure. She will begin talking sweetly to you and then stab you with a pin several times. Just when you think you can trust this very kind young woman, she stabs you again! She tattoos you with permanent reference points. The Glow Girls and the Hydra Herder seemed so nice, but I think Dr. Gargus has actually hired masochists for his technicians. There are now three blue dots that the machine and the Glow Girls will use to align my body properly for each session. I will get to carry those three blue dots for the rest of my life.

The Radiotherapy Center is designed to make you as comfortable as possible. Each morning you are met by a handsome and pleasant receptionist. All of the staff is truly caring and kind. The gowns are fabric, soft and large enough to cover you. The ceiling light in the treatment room is camouflaged with a picture of a blooming cherry tree limb. It is pretty and relaxing, except for the fact that you are really lying there having Flash Gordon death rays aimed at you. You don't feel any pain or heat. You just lie there being very still for what seems like hours but is only about fifteen to thirty minutes. The actually zapping takes less than the total time you are in position. The effects of the radiation will show up a few hours later as a sunburn. And yes, you do sometimes blister.

I have now been radiated, irradiated, irrigated, irritated and thank goodness I was not eradicated. My treatments will last for seven weeks or thirty-three sessions. During those seven weeks, my life changed forever. The cancer will only play a small role. The larger roles were the loss of my friend Ron and my mother.

Cancer was mostly an irritating factor, something with which I had to deal. Snell and I got up early every morning to feed Ramona through her tube and give the other cats their breakfasts.

Oh, I forgot to tell you. During this time, our son James brought home two flying monkeys, camouflaged as kittens. As if we didn't have enough going on, now we had two energetic critters added to our world.

Extra Crispy

W e make friends in odd places, don't we? I spent every morning for seven weeks with the same four women. If it was not for the coffee, laughter, and commiseration, I am not sure I would have made it. We'd have our coffee, laugh a little, commiserate a lot, and just share space together. It was amazing what sharing space with people can give you.

Each of us was dealing with cancer under our own unique circumstance. One woman brought her husband every morning for his radiation treatments. He was having chemo at the same time and was terribly tired. Truth was, so was his wife. Following a double mastectomy, Marquetta had chemotherapy. After that, she was in radiation treatment. Sheila was having the same type of radiation treatment as I for DCIS.

We developed a bond out of sadness, fear, and similar experiences. Most of the time you were standing in the cold dressing rooms together, half naked, and smearing aloe vera gel on various toasted body parts. All of us started within a few days of one another, and we all finished within the same ten-day period. As one person was passing through the doorway, we would hear "I got the machine all warmed up for you." Another common call was "Be sure to warm up your aloe vera. It is awfully cold back there."

I was nearing the end of my treatments, only four sessions left. The others knew Mama was ill and fading fast. My mama died on January 31. I came in on

February 1, and the three women looked at me as I just sat down. I didn't say anything. I couldn't. Snell and James had come with me that morning. Before Mama died, I would leave for the radiation center, come home, and then Snell would take James to work. That way we never left Mama alone.

Seeing my sad countenance, the woman who brought her husband asked, "What's happened?'

All I could do was say "Mama died last night."

Those words were all that was needed. We all knew about death from someone, and time was near for her husband. Back in the dressing area, each one of the staff, Marquetta, and Sheila hugged me. It was a very supportive moment. I am not sure I would have gotten through everything if those smiles had not greeted me every morning.

Several weeks after we had all completed our radiation therapies, we decided to get together to celebrate. We chose to meet for breakfast at the Main Street Restaurant. You get a bunch of women together who are celebrating having their boobies retextured, fried, and you might find some really giddy girls.

Everyone at Main Street figured out why we were there. We knew they would let us stay, laugh, and talk as long as we wanted to remain. We took pictures, measured Marquetta's hair growth, and discussed what we had been through, and what was going on in our lives at the present time.

Marquetta was returning to Pennsylvania to care for her mother. Our friend was caring for her husband, who lost his battle a few months later. Sheila continued to work and never told anyone that she had cancer or was in any kind of treatment. She kept everything to herself and her children. I continued to struggle with Mama's death, the death of my friend. and the care of our little Ramona. These three women helped me through some tough times. I honestly can't tell you how stressful and exhausting life was for me. Yet as they were supportive of me, they were going through their own battles.

You look for little achievements. Marquetta and John had the most serious of surgeries and treatments. Marquetta wore cute hats wherever she went, and she almost always had a smile. When her eyelashes became visible, we all celebrated. John would have a grin, a twinkle in his eye, and little joke for us most mornings.

"How's your suntan? Are you pink yet? Are you well done? Are you going for crispy or extra crispy this week?" We laughed and compared healing, scars, and quality of aloe vera.

We gave the doctors and staff points for warm, roomy cloth gowns and subtracted points for the room temperature. "Germs can't live in the cold." The nurses had told us. Apparently, cancer can't either. Since we are the hosts to cancer, we are freezing to death.

Sheila suggested baby bottle type warmers for aloe vera gel. We all cheered for her idea. I hope they finally did get something like that.

We have hashed through a lot of anger issues. Nothing makes you madder than having cancer. We have spent time crying and grieving together. We compared changes in our bodies. Yes, you have changes in color, textures, feeling, emotions, and in choosing the appropriate undergarments well after the last radiation treatment.

The three of us who had cancer all know that we are "cancer-free" for the moment. We don't know what the future holds, but we have each decided that we are not having it back!! Being positive in our healing and recovery is paramount to good health and attitudes.

I don't care how prepared you are when you enter a treatment center. You will always have trepidation. The three of us would be sitting there in the early hours of the morning. The staff with their smiles and a warm welcome were a soothing balm at times. Those smiles and those faces helped me through some trying times. I am very thankful for each of them.

True, we were all dealing with terrible circumstances. Our energies were low and our emotions high. We looked for the smallest pleasures. The joke of the day. Marquetta's eye lashes growing again. Our gentleman had been able to eat something the night before. Sheila laughing at something someone said. She has the best laugh. The greatest pleasure was bonding. It was meeting these women who got me through some of the toughest times of my life. I think I would have crumbled without their positive attitudes, along with Snell's strength and support. I felt like I just had to keep going.

The S.O.B.

I have been sick for several years. I can't tell you how many medical people I have seen or how many tests I have had. I have survived cancer. But, life, mother nature or some unnamed evil source decided to throw me another medical curve ball. Did you know that just before you pass out, everything becomes a nice soft blur? It is kind of pretty.

I am doing well now after having Nissen Fundiplication surgery to rebuild my esophagus. There was a lot of poking, prodding, and hyperventilation before Dr. Donald Dennis discovered that I was aspirating stomach contents into my lungs. There is a lot to tell about my experience with him, but first let me tell you about one of my early experiences before Dr. Dennis saved my life.

By the way, I left out the names of the various people involved in my earlier searches for improved health because most do not deserve any recognition. If you want the name of the doctor who told me that what I was experiencing was all in my head, call me. I will gladly give you my personal opinion, complete with flowery and fiery phraseology.

I was sent to several hospitals and medical offices for various and sundry tests. One test was for my SOB. I thought-- SOB?!? Sure, all of us have a little bitchiness in us, but how did he know mine was masculine instead of feminine? If a doctor had suggested such a test to my mama, she would've said, "That is a Sweet Old Boy test." My daddy would have probably slapped the doctor for saying that to him. And, I figured I probably dated the SOB at some time or another.

I know I probably shouldn't have, but I asked the person at the hospital registration, "How do you know if my SOB is masculine or feminine?" Very deadpan, the man said, "That's Shortness of Breath, ma'am." I was really tired by this time. Maybe I should not have asked the question. I was nearly dead. Gasping for breath and being the same color as bleached white towels are not my best choices of presenting myself and for meeting new people. Truthfully, the registration guy REALLY needed his SOB checked. I'm pretty sure his was masculine, but he needed some estrogen poured over it!

I have had almost every test known to man ---or woman. I've had the pleasure or displeasure of meeting an ENT with the personality of a dead possum. I met a very nice allergist who determined that I don't have asthma or allergies. After five—that's right FIVE—breathing tests, 300+ scratch tests, and a small period of unconsciousness, he determined that I have no problems with any kinds of pollen, mold, mildew, fungus, plant matter, or non-plant matter. The only thing he didn't check was food. That test had already been done by another doctor and showed no issues. If all else fails, I'll repeat the food allergies, but so far the internist, the allergist, even the ENT with less personality than worm fodder, all feel that food is not the issue.

I think the allergist just ran out of skin. After he breathalyzed me to near death, with and without various inhalants, he was scared to test anything else. Even as fat as I am, he used up all available square footage with his little pinpricks. After four hours in the office with him, I was starting to visualize this guy with Neptune's trident every time he came near me.

When all of those so-called experts had exhausted their bags of tricks, and the insurance company had probably said, "No more," I ended up with a pulmonary specialist. He is the one who ordered the SOB and a delightful morning of EKGs, EEGs, and cardio stress tests. I looked like I had lost a battle with an octopus. There were all these red suction cup "O"s all over my body.

That was quite a day. I had to be there at 6:30 and finally got called back at 8:30. Had no food or drink from 6 PM the evening before. This is not a great diet for losing weight. I thought, "As soon as I can eat, I am attacking anything that doesn't bite back."

The fun began: cardiogram and blood pressure standing, cardiogram and blood pressure sitting, cardiogram and blood pressure lying down. Then the walk of death. The good news...I did not fall off the treadmill. It did take the MD and two nurses to get me to the table. I was in full-fledged SOB though, and it was highly feminine. I would have used every nasty word I knew if I could have spoken. Then came a repeat of the whole exercise. I had five minutes of respite since I got off the treadmill. My eyes had not had time or energy to roll back in place from the top of my head, for heaven's sake. If I had had the strength, I would have grabbed that tiny, frail-looking doctor and sucked the life right out of him.

Afterwards I still couldn't eat, but the nurse said I could have a cup of coffee. Caffeinated. That's important in this little saga. I had to wait about ten minutes before I could have a PFT. (Aren't these little initials cute? Pulmonary Function Test). PFT is a better name because that is the only sound you can make after you have taken this delightful little exam. Just say it out loud, "PFFFFFT." I was told to breathe into the tube, suck from the tube, and blow into the tube until I see blackness and little stars starting to form. Repeat. In between this huffing and puffing, the technician is saying things like, "Blow harder, Honey. You're at 48%." "You can do better, blow, blow, blow..." This guy has the ultimate in expensive machinery for blowjobs.

Ah, the piece de resistance. Remember the coffee?

The guy gives me a nebulizer and tells me to breathe deeply, but normally. That's why I am here. I haven't had a deep or normal breath in two years! So, I take five minutes of hits off this white smoke. Then, he makes me blow into that infernal tube again. "Blow, honey, you can do it. More, blow, blow harder, blow." By now my legs are quivering, I have the headache from Hades, and I am becoming truly nauseated.

I had been locked into a small clear booth for these tests. The reason is not so that I can be observed; it is so that my body can't fall off the stupid little stool and lie convulsing on the floor. However, I just know that there was some smarmy little jerk behind the see- through mirror rating the redness of my face and saying, "Oh look, that purple cast means a #3 stroke has occurred in the left parietal lobe." I think they had a betting pool going. "Oh damn, I just wagered my month's salary on her having cardiac arrest within seven minutes. "

Well, the nebulizer contained two medications, which were the equivalent of six shots of highly caffeinated espresso. Remember the only thing I have had to eat or drink in more than fourteen hours is.......... a cup of caffeinated coffee. When I got home, I had the DTs for five hours. Sleep occurred only in seventeen-minute segments, and even then, I lay there jerking.

At least, this last batch of torture resulted in some explanations for my conditions. For some reason, the surrounding muscles are restricting the smallest bronchial tubes. That is what is causing the shortness of breath and general crappy feeling (highly technical medical term). The pulmonary specialist thinks it has to do with repeated pneumonia. I am to see another doctor on Wednesday. This one is going to "Possibly culture the sinuses and lungs." Don't they talk so nicely and genteelly? He is going to ram a probe up my nose and down my throat and rip out living portions of my body to place on his little Petri dishes. I am just so excited.

I am not sure modern medicine is going to be my answer. I am now interviewing witch doctors and voodoo priestesses. Save your chicken bones, rat claws, coon pellets, and possum gizzards. I am in need of a one-eyed snake caught under the light of a full moon, in a partial eclipse while you are eating a chocolate and strawberry pop tart, standing on your left foot with a raisin in your right ear. I understand that if I drink a brew made from this while the six-toed voodoo priestess rattles chicken bones, dehydrated owl eyeballs, and bat teeth in a counter-clockwise direction and chants, "Check the EKG, check the BP, and send in the SOB!" I will be cured.

The Mad Itch or I've Got Leprosy
Part I

Yesterday, I got up at 6:00 in the morning and looked like a bear hunting for a tree to scratch against! My entire body was covered in welts. Not a rash, but huge, bumpy things that were two and three inches across. Soon they all joined into one massive, itchy boo-boo. Even the soles of my feet were prickly. I went to the doctor as soon as she could see me.

The doctor said it was probably a reaction to one of my medications. The course of action was to determine which one was causing the problem. I was to stop taking all medications and supplements that were not essential. Once the rash healed, I could start adding one pill back every few days. I take several medications, one of which is an anti-homicidal pill. Let's hope my allergy was not a result of the last one. The doctor thought that my anti-homicidal pill was not essential. Boy was she wrong!

I was a delightful sight. There may have been a six square inch patch on my torso that was not a red welt. Do you remember the Stay Puff marshmallow guy from Ghostbusters? How just before he burst into flames, he was covered with blisters? Yeah, that was me, and I was not in as good a mood as he was.

LIFE IS HARD SOFTEN IT WITH LAUGHTER

Thank goodness for prednisone, Zyrtec, and Benadryl. I slept twelve hours after the Benadryl took effect. The doctor told me the prednisone would make me hungry. Such an understatement. I have eaten junk that I would not have looked at before this. I even bought candy corn, artificially colored sugar in a kernel shape. There is no nutritional value to candy corn. I ate a third of a bag before I got home. I don't eat after supper, that's dinner for you folks not from around here. Last night, I ate potato chips, chocolate, popcorn, chocolate, apples, chocolate, a whole gluten free pizza and chocolate. I was calling the whole thing supper and dared anyone to question me.

Fueling my hunger was not been the only side effect. My fashion had taken a hit. Gone were any clothing articles that would give a hint of my body shape. Anything that resembles a tent was now my fashion style. It was not to hide my figure but to prevent anything from touching my body. If something touched one of my spots, I itched, I scratched. I turned ugly.

My family had become wary of taking me anywhere public. I ws now categorized as VICIOUS due to the nearly closed eyes and drooling from my swollen lips. I'd heard the hushed description of rabid used to describe me.

I had taken prednisone before and knew it could make me a little antsy. The doctor put me on a triple dose for the first five days. She said I might be a little nervous or anxious. So far, I had washed and ironed everything, including a 108-inch linen table cloth and a second one that was only 96 inches long. Starched them, too. Stripped all the beds and washed all the linens, cleaned out a closet, pulled out clothes to go to the consignment shop next month. I also started cooking a pot of Irish stew and vacuumed the house. For those of you who know me cooking is not my favorite thing to do. And I had also eaten all the black jelly beans that I bought at the grocery store.

Tomorrow, I will take my third dose of triple prednisone. I am trying to make out my to-do list. First thing is to reorganize the panty. Oh, and clean the refrigerator for sure. As I do, I will try very hard not to eat everything in it. The upstairs needs a good organizing, too. Need to bush-hog. Perhaps paint the entire house.

You would think I would be losing weight with all this exercise and activity, but I am eating like I have just come off a ten-month famine. This is not good. And while I am working, I am getting hot. Hot is not good. I itch more when I get hot.

My house will be cleaner than the day before we moved in. You got two more days that I am on this level of medication. What do you need done? When I drop down to the normal dose, I will be exhausted and not worth killing. Get your requests in early. Remember, you have to feed me.

The Mad Itch or I've Got Leprosy
Part II

After all the prednisone and other medications, I got better. The rash seemed to have faded. And then............... Leprosy. My God, I've got leprosy. That was what it had to be. I woke up blind. One eye was completely closed, and the other could barely be wrenched open. My ears were swollen. My lips looked like I had a bright red banana split lengthwise down the middle. I could only make mmmmmmmmmmmFFFhhh sounds. My hands looked like baseball mitts. Shoes? You have got to be kidding me. My little piggies were not going anywhere.

I was Mrs. Potato Head!

Everything I had itched. Everything. From the bottoms of my feet to the top of my head, I was on fire. Even the inside of my ears itched unmercifully.

"Enough!" I had been to the dermatologist, internist, allergist, and the Emergency Room. Dr. Donald Dennis was one of the best doctors and diagnostician I have ever had the fortune to meet. Years ago, Dr. Susan Tanner and I were sitting next to each other at a luncheon. She had known I had been repeatedly ill with pneumonia. She told me to see Dr. Dennis, and I did. That was in 2005. He saved my life then and again when he, not any of the other doctors I saw, discovered I had acid reflux so badly that it had developed into a life-threatening issue. The specialists to whom he referred me gave me two years to live if surgery to rebuild my esophagus wasn't successful. It was. I lived.

When I called Dr. Dennis (AKA Dr. Darling), I was told to come in as soon as I could get there. Snell drove me to his office. When I walked in Valerie, the office manager and Tiffany, the receptionist said, in unison, "Systemic Candida." Okay, maybe I didn't need to pay for an office visit!

Dr. Dennis entered the exam room, glanced at me, and said "Systemic Candida." Now it is official. And it requires a co-pay.

After having Nissen Fundiplication surgery to repair my eroded esophagus, I was allowed to drink only Ensure like beverages for eight weeks. Then I got to add apple sauce and mashed potatoes for an additional four weeks.

Gradually, I added pureed baby food. I gag thinking about the baby food. Oh, the meat was the worst. I went strictly vegetarian and stopped most of the baby food. It was too dreadful. I no longer can throw up, and any attempts to do so could undo everything. I tried with the baby food. I really did, but I would get nauseated as soon as I smelled it. For eighteen weeks, I ate nothing but small amounts of lukewarm mush. Nothing hot. Nothing cold. Lost forty pounds and gained sympathy for babies.

What do these foods I chose to consume have in common? High carbohydrates. Carbohydrates convert to sugar. What does this do to your body? It provides the best possible environment for Candida (yeast) to thrive.

Yep, I was a loaf of rotten yeast bread! Eating this restricted diet for eighteen weeks before I was allowed to add regular textured food again caused this plague to set in. Prednisone only reduced the symptoms, not vanquished them. I will live the rest of my life on a high protein, low carb diet. If I get off and sneak something I shouldn't have, the welts return. I do the "My God, I've got leprosy" dance and eat anti-histamines like M & Ms.

Who knew that this type of reaction could happen? I surely didn't. I was diligent about eating only the softest foods. I didn't think about the carb content. It was an adjustment to the high protein diet. I have mostly gotten used to it. I haven't eaten wheat/gluten since 2005. I gave up sugar all together for years, and then I ate one piece of chocolate and wham! The addiction came back. Sugar is worse than cocaine. I guess that since I had given up sweets and breads once, I could do it again.

I am trying to be good, but dang! I'd really like to eat a grape.

The Wake-Up Call

This time last year, I was about to have an upper endoscope to determine what was wrong with me and my life force. The anesthesiologist sat down, took my hands into his and said, "We are going to keep you under for the minimum amount of time. I am turning your oxygen up a bit, and I want you take another hit off your inhaler just before we put under. I will be back to talk to you as soon as you are in recovery." OH, OK. The oxygen was whizzing through my head, and it was pretty good stuff. I hadn't breathed like this in a long time.

Then the surgeon, Dr. Smith, came in and sat down. He took both my hands into his and said just "Try not to worry. This is just to find out what we need to do. I will be back with you as soon as it is over." Well, both of those doctors had nice bed-side manners.

I had been fighting illness for several years. I had been exposed to some heavy-duty mold and mildew that had created a set of problems with my breathing and energy. My favorite doctor in the whole world, Donald Dennis, fixed that and told me not to eat anything gluten (wheat, barley, and rye) or fermented. I did what he said, and I got a lot better.

Then about two years ago, I started to have some more breathing issues. I was gasping and wheezing like a steam locomotive with a leak.

186

LIFE IS HARD SOFTEN IT WITH LAUGHTER

I kept going to various doctors for pulmonary issues and tests. No one could figure out what was wrong. I was put on and taken off all kinds of medications. I drank enough barium to float a battleship and was told I had a small hiatal hernia, but nothing of any concern. I took breathing tests until I fainted in the lab. Finally, Snell said to me, "Go see the man who fixed you the last time." So, I did.

Dr. Donald Dennis is one those amazing people who really wants to solve your problem. He wants to find an answer, and he wants everyone to be healthy. He is genuinely a great doctor and a good person. I know a goodly number of people who feel the same way as I do. I can tell you a multitude of stories of his generosity and kindness to others.

I called and made an appointment. I told Tiffany, the receptionist, that I was really struggling with breathing, and she said she could tell I was. She told me to wait a few minutes, and she would call me back.

Valerie, the office manager, was the one to call me back. She said Tiffany told Dr. Dennis how bad I sounded. He wanted me in the office first thing the next morning. So, the next morning, he and I had our hug fest. He started scoping my sinuses and throat. Yes, he squirts you with this numbing stuff and sticks his whole fist and head down your throat. No really, it was a little thin camera. 'Well, Marlene, I am going to take some pictures here. I just want you to see this."

Not to be too graphic, but if you want to see the pictures, I can show you, I had open lesions on my tonsils and vocal cords. I had bleached pathways to my right ear canal and sinuses from acid running from my stomach into my throat and head. I had stomach acid and stomach contents eating through the soft tissues of my innards. I was rotting from the inside out.

All of those other doctors had done tests and never bothered to look down my throat. I had acid reflux so bad that it had permanently scarred my lungs, esophagus, and bronchial tubes. I was not able to process an adequate supply of oxygen. No wonder I was exhausted after minimum effort. If I put on a good show and was out a lot for a day, it took me two days to recover. I was living on steroids and albuterol.

Dr. Dennis took charge. He got everything set up for me to see a specialist in pulmonology and esophageal issues and a surgeon. He told me I would need surgery to fix the extensive problems with my esophagus and fundus of the stomach. "I don't want you to be alarmed, but I am going to have to have some help on this. You are going to get better, but I need you to have several tests, and I want you to see these people." Dr. Dennis tried to sound reassuring and not setting off the already screaming alarms in my brain. I had survived cancer and prayed that was the end of anymore medical nightmares in my life. But life likes to throw curve balls and this one was a doozy.

Dr. Dennis called me at home several times to check on me. He would receive reports from the hospital and doctors and interpret them to me. I loved Dr. Dennis, AKA Dr. Darling.

Back to the recovery room. First Dr. Smith came in to give me his pep talk. "You are doing great." Have you ever noticed that you are always doing great, and then the BUT comes? "You are doing great, BUT you must have a surgery called Nissen Fundoplication to do these repairs. You have major, long term damage, and a simple surgery is not going to fix this." OK, Dr. Dennis told me this would not be a quick fix. Then Dr. Smith took my hands and said "Do you have all of your affairs in order? Just in case."

"WHAT? What did he say? Just in case of what?????" Dr. Smith went on to explain that the damage to my esophagus and lungs was causing me to have severe breathing issues. Scar tissue had formed in my lungs and esophagus and on other bits and pieces. In as nice and gentle way as possible, he told me, "Without this surgery and it being successful, you have maybe two years to live. Take care of your affairs before we go any further." I would have hyperventilated, but I couldn't get enough air.

Then the anesthesiologist came in. He pulled off his little bonnet, and his shiny head glared into my eyes. He sat down on the bed next to me, took both my hands into his, and looked into my eyes.

If you are in a hospital setting, never let anyone hold both your hands and look into your eyes. This is a HUGE red flag indicating bad news is on the way. He basically told me the same thing, but he added "Take care of all of your affairs and talk to your loved ones, now."

It really makes a difference in your life to be told by two doctors within fifteen minutes of each other that you are a dead woman in less than two years. I mean I had plans. I had to live one week longer than Snell and James, so I can be sure everything is taken care of as it should be.

Dr. Dennis called several times to check on me and give me all kinds of uplifting advice. I didn't announce things to the world, but I did try to talk to a couple of people who would need to be aware of things if something did happen. I was writing codicils to the will, identifying who would get what and trying to be sure all my business was in good shape for Snell and James. I did not try to scare anyone, but I did want a few people to understand that I was in dire straits. I don't think people really took me seriously, but I was not well and was truly getting worse every day.

I was scared, and Snell was scared but we kept it low-key because of James. I don't think my legal advisor ever really listened to the seriousness of my failing health. I was so frustrated.

When you can't breathe well, you feel like warmed over three-day old fish guts, and you have been told by three experts in their medical field to get your affairs in order you can get a little down in the dumps. When the buzzards start circling the house and people do not listen to the seriousness of what you are saying, you just have to determine that you are either going to make it or die trying.

When everything was over, Dr. Dennis told me just how severe my situation was. He said he didn't tell me everything because he didn't want me to get discouraged, but he and the other two doctors had quite a parlay.

None of them could believe I had the extensive internal rot going on and that the doctors were not sure I would wake up from the surgery or if they could do the repair necessary.

I am glad to say surgery was sixteen months ago. My surgery was more complex and complicated than many, but this surgery is done more often than you think. I have since talked to a couple of people who had it done. Gladly, I can report that all of us are doing well.

My outlook on life is much lighter. So, if someone in authority comes in and takes both your hands and looks you in the eye, pay attention and tell yourself "Hell no. I ain't going. I am going to get well."

When Did He Die?

The names of some of the people involved have been changed to protect the incompetents.

This is a true story. My husband's cousin, Charles, had been sick for a quite a long time. He died sometime in the early hours of January 6. That morning, when I couldn't reach him by phone, I went to his house to find him dead in his bed. I called the police so the process of a home death with no one in attendance could begin.

First, the city of Snellville fire-rescue team arrived, followed closely by the police.

Let me interrupt my story to say that all of these people were amazing. I am not a hysterical kind of person, but if I were, these are the professionals I would want around me. Each was competent, kind, and knowledgeable. They were amazing and took care of me and everything else. I was so pleased with their help, I sent them each a thank you note, written on real stationary and in cursive writing, no less.

When someone dies at home, the police notify the city or county coroner. This person will determine if the dearly departed will require an autopsy. Because I knew Charles' extensive health history, medications, and doctors, the coroner determined an autopsy would not be required. No autopsy meant Charles would be transported to the nearest hospital for date and time of death declaration.

Tom M. Wages' mortuary staff came out to claim our dear family member and took him to the nearest Emergency Room. The hearse doesn't even unload the body at the ER. A medical doctor comes outside to see the deceased, looks at his watch, and declares he has determined there is no life. The date and time are recorded. The whole process takes only a few minutes. Yeah, I know all this stuff. The things I know could be a bit scary.

Now, we get to the story. Charles' date of death was declared as January 6 at noon. For any reason one goes to the ER, even for a death declaration, a bill is generated. I have no problem with that. As the executrix of Charles' affairs, I took on the responsibility of his bills and other business issues. I called the local hospital's accounting office and requested all bills be sent to my address. Just to be safe, I checked his mailbox at least every other day, even though I had notified every business and completed a change of address with the post office.

The expected ER death declaration bill came. It was mailed to his home. I paid it. I included a comment that he had died on January 6, and any further correspondence should be directed to me.

Now, please realize Charles is dead. This ER is the one which declared him dead on January 6. It is very important to remember that he died on January 6, and the billing office has sent a bill for declaring him dead on January 6. And I have paid that bill.

Several weeks later, a duplicate bill was delivered to his house from this ER's accounting office. I called the accounting office. "Hello, I am Marlene Ratledge Buchanan, and I am calling on behalf of the late Charles Buchanan. The patient number is xxxx, and his date of birth is xx. I received a bill from the ER for services on January 6. I believe this is a duplicate. Please check your records that you received payment. "

"What was this for?"

I explained that it was to declare Charles dead. He had died at home without anyone in attendance.

"Oh, yeah (OH, YEAH? The teacher in me cringed). "He was dead. He didn't get any treatment?"

"No, Ma'am," I said, using my best Southern reply. "It was just to pronounce him dead. He died at home. Do you show the bill as having been paid? I received your bill on February 9 and mailed you a check, number xxx, by return mail."

"When did he die?" Being the polite person, I am, and before reaching levels of aggravation that would shake the chandeliers, I explained that Charles had died the morning of January 6. He had been brought by a hearse to the ER for a death declaration only.

"What day did you say?"

"January 6." I graciously repeated. The crystals were tinkling above the dining room table.

"He died on January 6. Was he in the hospital?"

"No, Miss Most Attentive. He died at home and was taken to the ER to be pronounced dead."

"Did he die on January 6? Oh, Yeah. It was paid."

"Thank you (for spending 25 minutes to determine this). Will you please be sure that the Accounting Department is notified, and this second bill is cleared?"

"Yeah, I can do that."

"Thank you for your help, Miss Sharp-as-a Tack. Have a good day." (I am going now to sweep the dining floor where the chandelier shook off a little glass.)

It gets better, folks. I swear, you cannot make this stuff up. On May 23, I received a bill from a collection agency. It was delivered to Charles' house. Thank goodness, I continued to check his mailbox until the new owners moved in. Now, if something came, the new family collected it and called me.

This was the only bill I had received since the duplicate in February. I pulled my copy of the original and duplicate bills. I had dealt with enough businesses and their representatives to know how important it was to record dates, beginning and ending times of a conversation, and the names of the people with whom I spoke.

I did my same shtick, "Hello, I am..., etc. I am calling about an unpaid bill I received from your company for Charles Buchanan's service at the local ER. His patient number, blah, blah, blah. The date of service was January 6, and it was to declare him deceased. I have paid this bill, I believe this one dated May 20 is an error."

"Yes, Ma'am. What can I do to help you?"

HMMMM. Did I not just explain why I was calling? "I received your notice stating that the bill for January 6 at the local ER had not been paid. I believe there is an error. On February 9, I received a bill for the January 6 service for Charles Buchannan, patient number xxxx. I paid it. A duplicate bill was sent. I talked to the accounting office. It was determined that the original bill had been paid, and the duplication error was supposedly cleared up." Simple. Succinct.

"UH-huh. What date was it for?"

"January 6."

"What was his patient number?" I provided the number again, his date of birth, again, the full spelling of his name, again. And, are you ready, his date of death, again.

"What was this for?" Dang, there went those crystals dancing again.

"Charles died at home. This was for an ER doctor to declare date and time of death."

"Was he admitted to the hospital?" Clink and a clunk replaced the occasional tinkling.

"No, he was not. The doctor just had to declare he had passed away."

"What day did he die?"

"January 6." There was the first sound of glass hitting Mama's dining room table.

What kind of treatment did he get at the hospital?"

"None. He was not admitted. The doctor declared him dead, and he released the mortuary van to leave with Charles' body."

"He was dead?"

"Yes, he was dead." Clink, tinkle, crack with an upgraded rhythm from a slow sway to heavy rocking.

"What day did he die?"

At this point, the whole chandelier was swaying in the blue smoke coming from my ears. I always use these people's names. This time I was using her name many times trying to get her to follow along with me. I was also using her name in vain in my head.

Patiently, but with gritted teeth, I ask, "What do you need to close this account? Charles died on January 6. The bill was paid on February 9. His estate has been finalized, and all other affairs settled. Do you want me to mail you a death certificate?" At this point I was afraid I was going to have to produce the body.

"Yeah, a death certificate. We need something telling us what day he died."

Tinkle, clink, crash.

Bush Hogging My Way to Happiness

It is that time of the year again. The April showers have certainly brought spring flowers--- and grass and weeds.

There are not many things I enjoy more than getting all dressed up in my garden finery and bush hogging. I know you are jealous because you don't have the best wardrobe like mine or a tractor that is the same age as you. If you come by the house and want to go skinny dipping, I have a mismatched pair of boots at the bottom of the pond you can retrieve for me.

For you that do not know what bush hogging is, let me try to explain. You ride a tractor and you pull a wide, flat lawn mower type thingy behind you. If all goes well, it cuts down everything that gets into its path. If things don't go well, you yell, scream and call Snell to come fix it.

Telling you about my lovely pair of boots brings me to a different and not truly related tale. Golf carts do not float No, do not try this at home. I have; they don't. They do ricochet off walls and can fly about six feet before hitting the water. The fish don't like the invasion and it ticks off Chi-Chi, the turtle. Then you have to swim out, get chains and the tractor, swim in again, dive under water to connect the chains, and drag the cart out. Fishing a golf cart from a pond is not a fun way to spend a couple of hours, and it leaves you with mismatched boots.

LIFE IS HARD SOFTEN IT WITH LAUGHTER

My friend, Paul Dickson, and I were talking online one day about our tractors. His is a relatively new one, only forty or fifty years old. Paul asked me if I used a chain saw and did all kinds of yard work. I had to tell him that I could no longer use the gasoline chain saw, but Snell and James gave me an electric limb trimmer and an electric chain saw for my birthday. I am now a woman of mass destruction. I think he thought I was a prissy little thing, but I'm not.

Back to my story. I love to bush hog. I like messing in the flowers, but I LOVE to bush hog. There is a sense of accomplishment. You can look back over your shoulder and see this wide swath of weeds that you have mown down. You can look forward to all your antagonists (goldenrod, poison ivy, trash grass) and know you are about to annihilate them.

We have lots of those tall dandelions, wild asters, and daisies. I cut around those clusters. The yard looks a little patchy, but that's okay. The pretty flowers stay, and I get to play in the yard on my toy of choice.

Things I love about bush hogging are simple. Only one person can be on the tractor. You can pretend you don't hear anyone calling your name. If someone starts trying to find you, you can drive up behind the pine grove and cut your neighbor's yard. He is appreciative, and you are out of sight for a time.

Not many things can stand in your way when you are bush hogging. Animals and insects scurry away. I have taken out small trees with that thing. I have trained my family that this is my time of meditation. I can work out problems on that tractor. I can pretend I am running over my enemies with it. I can cry, and no one knows it. I can scream as loud as I want, and no one hears me. I can laugh, and no one can tell I am hysterical.

We all need mental therapy every once in a while. Mine is cheap. A couple of gallons of gasoline, and I am good for hours.

Stop by the house anytime. You may need a shovel to get through the front door, but you are welcome. If I

am on the tractor though, you best keep going. I can't
see you or hear you.

Nature

"Mama had a very specific scream. It was the-worm scream. I inherited the scream from Mama. Mine is reserved for spiders."

Where were You When I needed Your Expertise

I have a couple of friends who could not possibly live with my son James. One is Marie Beiser. She and I worked together for many years at Parkview High School. She and her husband Bob are James' godparents. I'd better out live them because there will be trouble if James has to move in with them.

Marie doesn't like crickets, frogs, or other things that creep and crawl. James, however, loves them all. I have almost learned not to have a stroke at the sight of a spider or snake. But crickets, worms, lizards, frogs, and other things like them don't bother me.

The senior class prank at Parkview one year was to release thousands, perhaps millions, of crickets into the main school building where our offices were. Bartow Jenkins and Ed Hunt, principal and assistant principal respectively, always got there early. They were well trained in the knowledge of senior class pranks and teenage exuberance in general.

On this particular morning, they found crickets in every conceivable space in that school. They called in other staff and began sweeping and vacuuming up crickets like crazy. Crickets do not stand still and let you catch them. They jump, crawl, and bounce. Catching a thousand crickets in a single room would be an impossible task to say nothing of the hordes of crickets bouncing around the high school that morning.

By the time I got to work, the crickets were mostly corralled with a few showing up in odd places. Marie decided she had to go to the bathroom. We only had one female faculty bathroom in our building. On the way out the door, she suddenly stopped. She came back into the office and asked me to go to the bathroom with her.

Now, we were beyond the age of adolescence where teenage girls go to the bathroom together to primp, giggle, and talk about people; however, she would have peed in her pants before going in there without someone surveilling the territory for cricket snipers. I was the Mighty Rescue Power Ranger. Yes sir! There I was in panty hose, a dress, and high heels crawling around on the floor to catch crickets so Marie could come in the bathroom. What are friends for? Apparently, I was a better friend than a representative of MENSA because I was the one on the floor with a cup of crickets.

And then, there was our friend Kim. Early one morning she went into her kitchen, just minding her own business. She turned to put something onto the counter, and there, staring at her was a frog. The frog was approximately twenty-five pounds, two feet high and was humming "Kimmmm" under its breath. The truth was it was a tree frog about two inches high. At that moment, it didn't matter. Her son's name is Bobby. Bobby, who was soundly asleep as only an innocent teenage boy can was blasted from his bed by the shriek that cracked every mirror in the house.

Running down the stairs and expecting to find his mother massacred all over the kitchen, he found her pointing at the tree frog. "Get it! Get it! Get it!" was all she could say. Bobby calmly picked the frog up and walked outside. Kim was shivering from seeing the frog and knowing her son actually touched that vicious beast.

Then her husband came in and asked what is going on. Kim was trying to stutter out about the giant frog on the kitchen counter when he said, "It was a good thing I had to go to the bathroom before you got up. I found one sitting on the toilet seat." Kim almost fainted. Not only had a frog touched the very seat upon which she had so recently perched, but her husband had not bleached the seat after removing said varmint. Kim's whole house smelt like Clorox. You have to be certain nothing has become attached to your clothing like a bug or a frog when you enter her house.

And then there was Mama. Mama had a very specific scream. The Worm Scream! It really wasn't a scream limited to just any worms. It was more for worms that hung from trees. The ones that land on you. Big, no huge, no really GIGANTIC hairy caterpillars. Daddy got to the point where he would hear the scream, walk over with clippers, cut the beast in half, and go back to what he was doing without blinking an eye. Once the critter was deceased, Mama returned to what she was doing, just as calmly as if nothing had happened.

I inherited The Scream from Mama. Mine is reserved for spiders. Snell and James do me the same way Daddy did Mama. James scoops up the offensive hideous critter and carries it off far away from me. Snell just says. "It's a spider. Let me know when it gets close." Sigh.

Recently I received an email from Marie asking, "Where were you when I needed your expertise?" Oh dear.

She explained in her email that she was getting ready to take a shower when she saw "a grey looking spot on the back of the toilet top where her towels are stacked. The grey thing was on part of the porcelain at the bottom of the towels. "So, I touched it to pick it up, for it reminded me of when I clean the lint from the washer and leave the lint ball up on the top of the dryer. Lo and behold, it jumps up. It's a small frog."

Now, I know Marie, and when she said she "called out for Bob," was an understatement if I ever read one. She used the Frog Scream alert vocal cords. Bob got in there as fast as he could. He thought Marie was being slaughtered by a maniac in the bathroom.

They couldn't find the frog. Fluffy, the cat, spent the day in the bedroom and bathroom on high alert, but the frog never made a second appearance. At least, not until Marie had all her clothes off and was "buck-naked." Her email continued to describe her second encounter with their new house guest, "I peeled off all my clothes to put on my pajamas. When I picked up my pocketbook on the bed, the frog hopped again. This time he was on the bed."

Once again, I was sure Marie calmly called out for Bob to go get the bucket. He came to the rescue with paper towels and a bucket. He caught the frog and placed him outside. All was safe now, but Fluffy was a bit ticked off, for she has been on guard duty all day and had her taste buds set for frog.

So, to all of those unsung heroes who rescue people from the vicious beasts like crickets and frogs, I salute you. Torn panty hose and all. After all what are friends for?

Mother Nature Hates Me

Well, I found another big yellow jacket nest yesterday.

"What?" you say. "How could you be so lucky?"

I just am, I guess. That makes the second one in eight days. Now, all I have to do is stand in the yard, and they will come, pop me fast and furiously and depart to get all their family and friends to come back.

My yellow jacket dance is almost as pretty as my spider dance. The Spider Dance has its own scream, which makes it much more impressive. The yellow jackets just get yells of "Damn, damn, damn" and a hopping-running thing. Nothing as elegant as the twisting and turning of the Spider Dance. The Spider Dance is a complete aerobic work-out in less than one minute.

I am working on a yellow jacket scream, though. It will be much more effective than the cussing. Screams carry farther.

The Yellow Jacket Dance may just have to be what it is. Slapping and running. "Damn, damn, damn."

If you smash one, they put out a scent calling all the family into battle. There must be a hive of the things that covers a least an acre. The nests have three openings. One main one, one back door, and a hidden escape hatch. Those beasties are fast, too. You see only one, but there are hundreds waiting in the bushes to get you.

My reactions are so much worse. I don't know if it is age or my histamines are shot due to other stressors in life. I don't recover like I used to do. My knee looks like a small cantaloupe and doesn't bend without pain, so I am having trouble walking this morning. I can't put on anything with a waist band, either. I must have gained three inches around my middle from the welts.

Tell me how yellow jackets can get under clothes to attack? Those things got me under my tucked in shirt. My socks were pulled up over the hem of my pants, but that didn't keep them out. How did they get into all of these nooks and crannies of my body? I was tearing off my clothes while running and yelling. On the inside of my shirt were yellow jackets. Good thing we live a ways off the road, and my neighbor wasn't out! It was not a pretty sight.

I think I have gone too long to reclaim my yard! Nature wants it back. All these years I have been sick, she has been able to take care of things—HER way. So now, she is sending her battalions of warriors (yellow jackets, spiders, snakes and other valiant beings) to warn me off her terrain.

I think she has won.

Wisteria Goes Postal

One of the most beautiful flowers on earth is the wisteria, and one of the sweetest fragrances is also the wisteria. This vine has long clusters of flowers that bloom in purple, white, or pink. The purple flora is more common in our area. Wisteria is a member of the pea family and native to the south eastern United States, China, and Korea.

Wisteria is also one of the fastest growing climbing vines in the world. It rivals Kudzu in heartiness. The plant puts out runners, anchoring its viney limbs with roots. Once it reaches a tree, it zooms up to the top. It is so strong that it can distort the growing trunk and limbs of trees. It is ruthless. Wherever it wants to go, it grows.

Just drive down roads with old woods and abandoned houses during the month of May. You will see huge trees devoured in the wisteria vines, heavy with scent and flower. It is luscious. You want to bury your face in one of those beautiful pods of flowers and breathe in the glorious fragrance, but I advise against such an impulse. It might think you are a tree, and you will go home dressed in purple and really smelling good. It is reported that wisteria can climb as high as sixty to seventy feet above the ground and can spread about thirty feet laterally. According to Wikipedia, the world's largest known wisteria is located in Sierra Madre, California. It measures more than one acre in size and weighs about 250 tons. The one growing on my mail box would be larger than that if Mama and I didn't keep attacking it with the pruning shears. We have found runners that could double as rope and thriving more than fifty feet from the main plant.

A carefree plant with few demands, it needs no fertilizer. I think it requires only a place to grow, sunlight, and a body to climb. I don't believe it even needs water. The mysterious wisteria never seems to wilt in the summer heat and drought. The hearty plant is just green and keeps on growing.

One of the many things I have done wrong in my life, perhaps the greatest sin, was to plant an old-fashioned wisteria to climb an arbor over the mailbox. Mama and I really do keep it trimmed. It just grows five feet or more every night. The tendrils of steel twist and turn as they gracefully reach out. We whittle on it at least weekly. I have taken a weed eater and cut it back to within an inch of its life. The next morning it was fully bushed.

I would like to apologize to our mail person for my whimsy of thinking wisteria would be a beautiful asset to our home. The problem is the mail people keep getting replaced. I don't know what is happening to them, although I did find a US Postal worker patch in the top of the wisteria arbor recently....

Possum or Opossum

"They are not bad critters, especially with sawmill gravy" (Steve Butler).

Recently, Jim O'Neal, retired Brookwood High School teacher, mentioned on Facebook a raccoon had attacked one of his dogs. The raccoon tested positive for rabies. Even with up-to-date rabies shots, the dog will still receive some treatment and must be observed regularly. This discussion led to something that my son had told me about possums or Opossums if you aren't from around here.

The body temperature of a possum is too low for it to become infected with the rabies virus. As a matter of fact, a possum carries few diseases for this reason and is one of the healthiest wild animals we have. That doesn't mean you want to go out and engage one in play.

This Facebook conversation led to much discussion of the cuteness vs. ugliness factor of possums. (I say possum, I am from around here.) Some say that possums are so ugly they are cute. Daddy said opossum should be OH! Possum for

OH!
Possibly
Orneriest
Suspicious
Sucker
U
Meet

LIFE IS HARD SOFTEN IT WITH LAUGHTER

A possum is an ugly varmint. Some people say not even the Mama Possum can stand to look at her babies in the face. That's why she carries them on her back.

Robert O'Neal thinks they look like George Jones. And Joe Beck's grandmother says they are better ratters for the barn than any cat. They eat insects, worms, and some other things that we don't want to know about. I lean toward thinking they are on the cute side. Granted when they show their teeth some of their appeal diminishes, but basically, I think they are cute. Opossum orthodontics hasn't really caught on. Melinda Henley Wharton said she thought they were cute until one hissed at her. Y'all do know that hissing is just their way of saying "Hey there, Sweet Thang." All possums speak with a southern twang.

Several people suggested possum recipes from Granny Clampett of Beverly Hillbillies fame. Apparently roasted with veggies is preferred to boiling in a stew. Possum with baked sweet potatoes is considered a delicacy for Sunday dinner. Not at my house, just in case any of you really want to know.

Possums are marsupials like kangaroos. The young are born and make their way through Mama's fur to the pouch where the nipples are. They live there until they are a pretty good size and then they crawl out to ride on Mama's back. Many of the possums who are killed are carrying babies in the pouches.

A number of people commented about rescuing the babies from a killed mother's pouch. Apparently, they made good pets when raised from an early age. Bonny Ragsdale Rosser has a good friend who is known as a possum whisperer. She is a lover and supporter of all things possum. She has rescued and raised two of them. Once raised, I guess you have to keep them inside because they wouldn't know how to live in the wild. (Please tell me they are litter box trained.) Michael Gary Barker says he feeds his "barn cats and barn possums" cat food.

A possum is slow and would prefer to curl up and play dead to fighting. I wish more people were like that. If forced into a battle, a possum has some pretty wicked teeth and claws. It can really injure another animal.

Mama and Daddy had a pet door that was closed every night so the dog and cats couldn't go out after dark. One night, the dog woke up everyone in the neighborhood. A possum that lived in the back woods came up at night to eat persimmons. This night the pet door was accidentally left open, and the varmit came right on in. It was eating the dog food when my parents found it. The critter dropped to the floor and played dead, even with the dog after it. The possum was brighter than the dog, which isn't saying much for either one of them.

You would have sworn it was dead. No signs of breathing. Daddy put on welding gloves and picked it up, relocating it to the base of the persimmon tree. It lay there until Daddy was back in the house. Then, it got up and started eating the fruit like nothing had happened. No hissing, fighting, or anything, just docile. Mama said the possum did look back over its shoulder and gave the dog a "nanny-nanny-pooh-pooh" smirk though.

It really doesn't matter if you think they are cute or not. We are in the land of possums, and here we have to live together, but apart. I will share my son's favorite joke with you. Do you know why the chicken crossed the road? To show the possum that it could be done!!

Muskrat Love

James loves animals. All kinds. When he was little, before kindergarten age, he knew all the dinosaurs and other animals by name, genus and species. He could tell you way more than you ever wanted to know about the inner workings of a critter.

We read all the children books, Dr. Seuss and the Bernstein Bears. His favorite was the *Zoo Books*, a magazine for kindergarten and older children. He had us read those pages so often he learned all the material. Even at this age, a grown man, he will watch a nature show over anything else.

During the summers James attended the Busch Garden's Zoo Keeper camps. The first time he went, he was working behind the scenes where the large cats are kept. Cauliflower and Lilah were two female tigers who were resting away from the public. James worked beside their space during that visit. He started talking to them. Cauliflower went over to him and lay down by the fence. James kept talking. Shortly, Lilah came over and sat next to them. James was scratching these giant white tigers through the fence openings while talking to them both.

If any of the instructors came over, the two tigers stood up and hissy-growled. When the instructors moved back away from James, the tigers lay down. James spent most of the day with those two giant felines. No one could believe it. The staff let him be with Cauliflower and Lilah for the day. James was given permission to visit the "pretty little girls" every day. The tigers always greeted him and rubbed up against the fence so he could tickle their ears and be loved on. He has that touch with animals.

The next year that he attended, the instructors decided he needed to be in a more advanced group. He was still in high school, but the instructors placed him in the course for the zoology students at University of Florida took for credit. The director told us James would have gotten an A if he had been enrolled in the college course.

Right now, I want to tell you about the muskrat. One morning, when James and I were leaving our house, he saw an injured muskrat just beyond our driveway. Do you know what a muskrat looks like? A fifteen-pound water rat, complete with the long hairless tail. I had traffic stopped on both sides of the road. James was trying to encourage the semi-conscious muskrat to stagger toward me. The plan was I would try to pick the poor thing up with a thick insulated bag. While the muskrat and I sort of wandered and staggered into the middle of the street, James phoned his daddy and told him to come help.

James was setting up triage procedures for healing that varmint. He gave his daddy explicit instructions. If the muskrat was fatally wounded, Snell was to put it out of its misery. AND then freeze it. If it was OK, Snell was to put it into a box and give it a little bowl of water, but no food for several hours. He told Snell, "You have to be careful with concussions."

Snell doesn't hear well, and he gets practically nothing from a cell phone conversation. He thought James was saying something about a rat, but he wasn't 100% sure. Snell was wondering why we were trying to save a rat. Well, Snell and I wonder a lot about the things James tries to save. Snell came loping up our long driveway where I am standing in a pale pink suit and pink open toed sandals. I have an insulated bag wrapped around this huge rodent when the muskrat regains full consciousness. He started to wiggle, and I started to panic.

James began yelling, "Don't drop him! Give him to me!" I am dancing and screaming, "It's ALIVE! " in front of five or six cars. The muskrat looked me the eye. I swear, directly in the eye. I could hear its little brain telegraphing the message "Put me down, NOW." I did. I continued to shimmy and shake the muskrat's cooties off me.

James is calmly saying "Let me get him. Daddy, get a box."

Snell is yelling "Let it alone. It is OK."

"No, Daddy, it's bleeding. It has a concussion."

Yep, we are the neighborhood entertainment. You might also note that not one person got out of their car to help an old woman and a young man with an injured muskrat.

The muskrat got away from all of us. Only James was sad about that. He was trying to follow it into the huge drainage pipe that comes under the road. Finally, Snell persuaded James to go with me in the car, and good Daddy that he is, Snell dutifully combed the area. The muskrat was nowhere to be found.

Six months later Snell confessed to some friends that all he heard from James was RAT and freeze it. He said he had no plans to save a rat, let alone freeze the dang thing. He just wanted to be sure that James wouldn't find it when we got back home.

I can't believe some of the things we do.

Pull Over Ma'am

I was notorious in the city of Atlanta for driving like a banshee on a mission, but I got better about that. Snell said I drove like I had a blue light and a siren on my car. Well, the person that taught me to drive was an Atlanta policeman, so maybe there is some truth to his description.

On more than one occasion, I have been pulled over on I-20 coming from Carrollton to East Atlanta. I was lucky though. I never got a ticket, but I did get a few warnings. "Patsy, if you don't slow down, I am going to call your daddy."

Daddy always knew about it before my car made it home, anyway. "Slow down, Patsy. You are going to kill yourself or somebody else."

The knowledge of not being invincible has helped my lead foot. Being invincible is a disease of youth, you know. How many young people have paid a price for the youthful blind faith that "it won't happen to me"?

I have slowed down, and I do put on brakes much further away than seven feet from the stop sign. Yellow lights no longer mean speed up and rush through the intersection. Caution has been exercised. I have stopped pushing the limits of my youthful stupidity.

However, last week I met a young man who is a Gwinnett County policeman. I was driving sedately along the road from my house. My speed was with the flow of traffic and well within the legal speed limit. Suddenly, I

214

jerked the wheel to the right and took a turn into a subdivision on two wheels. The stench of burning rubber and clouds of blue smoke poured from my tires.

I jumped from the car and started the Comanche War Dance, complete with afore mentioned banshee screams of death, destruction, and terror. I didn't stop when the policeman, with his blue light twirling, pulled up behind me. He even did a whoop-whoop with the siren. I know he thought he was going to have to call for back-up and the insane asylum van.

Well, the blue light and the whoop-whoop didn't help at all. Maybe, if I had his gun...

Do you all know what a wolf spider is? It is a big, hairy spider that probably spans the size of a fifty-cent piece. I was driving along and saw one sitting on my right leg, looking at me. Smiling at me. I think there was a little bit of drool coming from the corner of its mouth.

What would you do? I thought I handled the situation well. One spider scream, I got off the road and leaped from the car. I could have set Olympic records with the sitting to standing long jump. That spider was the size of a saucer, weighed at least a half-pound, and was looking at me.

Wolf spiders can jump. They often capture their prey by jumping on it. The dang (expletives deleted and trust me there were plenty of expletives in use) thing was sitting in my lap and looking at me. I am pretty fat and would probably have been a good meal for this one-pound, dinner-plate sized spider. But, he had to catch me first.

When I hit the pavement, I did a shimmy that would make your Sister Kate green with envy. (Yeah, I'm old. My references are old, too. Google it.) I may get bills for replacement windows because I let out one of my famous Spider Screams that might have cracked some glass.

I don't know who was more frightened, me, the spider, or the cop. The policeman was pretty wide-eyed, and I was not a calm, sedate old woman. I did all my aerobic exercise for the month in that one minute.

"Ma'am?" I hate being old enough to be called a ma'am, but it is better than the alternative. I was pretty sure that three-pound, platter-sized wolf spider was going to kill me. I might have killed myself with a massive heart attack, and he would have had a big old feast of quivering cholesterol lying right there on the street.

"Spider!" That was the only discernible word that came from my mouth. Well, "$%&(*^$$&* spider!" might have been understandable. The policeman looked at me like I was nuts. Then he jumped back and let out an expletive deleted himself. He saw it.

"That is the biggest spider I have ever seen!" He had his hand on his holster. He might have been going for the stun gun, but I really am not sure there were enough volts to stop that monster.

By this time, I had begun to breathe normally. The policeman and I just looked at each other. We started to laugh. Both of us were standing in the street laughing and crying. Apparently, the spider thought we were too dangerous to be around and crawled off to parts unknown.

"I understand and don't blame you," the officer said as he started to return to his car.

I smiled at him and said "Thank you. You should have shot him but thank you for stopping to check on me. Look in your car before you get in it. You left your door open."

Laughing, but with caution, both of us did a thorough search of our vehicles before we drove off, smiling and waving at one another.

The spider is stalking another neighborhood. I am not going to tell you where.

Fashion and Travel

"Gaudy is not just a fashion statement, but an important state of mind."

Hot Trend

Every twenty years or so, there is a major influence in fashion. Every fifty years, it is mega-major. I hit the one in the 1960's. I grew up in one of the most powerful fashion eras of all times. The Sixties. We wore Daisy Dukes before there was a Daisy Duke. Hot pants, yep, Mini-skirts, the shorter the better. Bold eye makeup. Braless, well, yeah. We now have a generation of old women with Copper's Droop due to the braless trend. But, we were hot stuff then.

Think about what Flappers did for fashion in the 1920's. The success of those freely moving dresses and ta-tas was the result of Mary "Polly" Phelps Jacob. In 1913, Ms. Polly was dressing in the whale bone corsets/girdle/Iron Maiden required for all women. Those nineteen-inch waists, so popular with Scarlett O'Hara and others, was not natural. They were sutured into waist cinchers and other garments designed by men for what men wanted to see: An hourglass figure, big on top, big on bottom.

Ms. Polly had a new gown. She was a wild and brazen twenty-two-year-old with a High Society pedigree and the money to back her whims. Once laced into the knee to arm-pit whalebone corset, her maid dropped her

218

new gown over her head. "Oh, NO." Cried Ms. Polly. "I am not perfection. You can see some of the staves at the neckline of my gown. Oh, what to do? What to do?"

You probably know what she did. She took two linen handkerchiefs and pinned them together, forming two triangles. She, more likely the maid, stitched on a piece of ribbon at the apex of each triangle and at the outside point. Ms. Polly tied on that piece of linen and shouted, "Let them be FREE." And honey, that is when the world went to hell in a handbasket. Well, according to some. To most women, that was the beginning of being in charge of one's own self. Once the "girls" were free, other womanly ideas soon followed.

Those men who designed the whalebone torture chamber didn't like this new-found freedom of the "girls", but those men dancing with the bone-free, newly released ta-tas were all for it. The new backless brassiere still maintained a flattened-chest image, but the comfort of the design "was delicious" Jacob wrote in her memoir, *The Passionate Years*. She went on to patent her design.

Her backless brassiere made movement possible. It also allowed for bad posture which the whalebone corsets did not. Even dancing became freer. From the stiff and formal dances of the waltz and foxtrot to the free-swinging Charleston and the delectable Tango. Can't do that backbend in the tango in staves.

And then came Katharine Hepburn. In the late 1920's and early 1930's, Katharine Hepburn and Marlene Detrick were seen wearing trousers in public. It was not an easily accepted style. Androgynous was the term used for those daring females, and that was the nicest of the descriptive terms. Around 1933, Hepburn had begun wearing pants in movies. In almost every movie she made, she wore trousers at some point. *Philadelphia Story*, in 1933, was the exception. Her character had to have a certain presence, and Hepburn felt pants were not the appropriate choice.

Women loved it. Men kind of liked the look from behind, too. They had better like it. Pants were here to stay.

Skirt length varied through the years. During World War II, fashion became more restricted, but then so did life. Skirts got shorter, though. Why, you ask? Because the world was using available resources to support fighting for others and maintaining our freedom. Cloth used for long skirts was an expense. Shorten the skirt and save money and material. You will notice in WWII, more "dress outfits" had a tailored, closer to the body straight skirt. Only house dresses really had the fuller skirts so women could work in them. More importantly, women went to work in factories that required closer fitting clothing: PANTS.

Well, Ms. Hepburn showed that it was OK to wear pants in public. Women realized that working in pants was not only safer and more comfortable but gave a freedom of movement like no other. They could play, not in prim tennis whites, but in rough and tumble jeans. They didn't have to change clothes to leave the house; they could go out in their pants.

This sense of freedom hit a new movement in the late 1940's and 1950's. Rock and Roll and Boogie Woogie really came into fashion. Boys were coming home from war. They had all the restrictions of military life and death threats they wanted. They wanted to move. They wanted to laugh. They wanted to swing.

Money was more available. Material for skirts allowed women to make the big circular skirts we see in old movies. Those skirts, like the pants, allowed for the jitterbug dancing. Seeing those full skirts, created by yards and yards of crinolines, gave women the hourglass figure back. Big on top and big on bottom. Remember that favorite from long ago? Tight little waists, torpedo boobs, and full swinging hips.

Let's fast forward to the 1960's and 70's. Viet Nam War was cranking into high gear. Young people became more verbal and, unfortunately, more violent. Many were protesting what they didn't always understand or understood all too well. They were fighting the violence of war with violence of their voice and actions. Suddenly, color burst forth. Not soft colors, but vivid, screaming colors. Bold, angry, outspoken colors and patterns that blasted forth like explosions.

Men and women began to use color to call attention to themselves in ways never seen before. Cuts of clothing became more textured and vibrant. All this reflected the youths' voice of "see me, hear me." People began experimenting with shapes and fit. Tighter clothes, shorter clothes. Shorten the skirt, lengthen the boot. Deep plunging neck lines and long flowing skirts. Less restriction in clothing was representative of thoughts in some ways. Was it more or less restricting in the way people reacted to others?

Fashion is a reflection of our lives. Sometimes it is a good reflection and sometimes not so good. All I can really say is "God bless you, Polly Phelps Jacob. You started it all."

Tasteful Native Costumes

Shortly after Snell and I married, we agreed to chaperone the graduating class of Duluth High School on a cruise to Nassau and Freeport. We had a stop in Puerto Rico for an evening, and a bunch of the boys wanted to go into the port. They didn't feel comfortable enough to go by themselves, so they approached us about going with them.

We agreed and went to the concierge's desk to find out what was available in town. There were very few choices, but the concierge told us about an upscale dinner show. It sounded wonderful. The dancers performed folk dances in tasteful native costumes. That sounded safe enough. He suggested we take a taxi, so we wouldn't get lost.

The boys all went back to their rooms and dressed in coats and ties. Snell and I got all duded up and met the guys at the debarkation ramp. We hailed a taxi to head into town. This was the first time for any of us to ride in a taxi, and all of us were crammed inside the vehicle. I think there were either six or eight of us. We were off on a great adventure of firsts. I was in Snell's lap, and the boys were mushed up together. Lots of excited laughter flowed from the taxi's windows.

The first thing the taxi driver told us was not to walk around on the streets. He said to have the restaurant call for a taxi before we went outside and then go out only to get into the car. OKAY. Maybe going into Puerto Rico to this nightspot wasn't such a good idea. Snell and I had a bunch of seventeen and eighteen-year-old young men with us, and we were headed into an area of such disrepute that even the taxi driver warned us away.

Well, we went through some interesting parts of town. We saw lots of people lounging against old cars. Many were smoking and drinking from shared bottles. Several young and not-so- young women were, ummmm, there, too. The boys were quick to point out the various makes and models of the old vehicles, and, thank goodness, they didn't pay a lot of attention to the, ummm, entertainment that the men and women seemed to be, ummm, having in and around the cars.

Yes, we were driving a bunch of innocents into the heart of the den of iniquity.

We arrived at the restaurant, which was brightly lit and was very attractive on the outside. The interior, however, was nearly as black as the innards of a buzzard. After we cut through the smoke and were seated, we had a good vantage point facing the stage. We were placed at a long table, not across from each other but side by side. We assume the purpose was because the floor show was so good that the restaurateur didn't want the audience to miss a minute of the artistry of the folk dances and tasteful native costumes.

All of us were excited, laughing and talking together. None of the boys nor myself had ever been to a real live floor show. We didn't know what to expect, but the meal was good, and the music playing was quite nice. Then, drum roll, the show began. The audience lights dimmed even more. If it hadn't been for the people at the next table smoking like chimneys, we would not have been able to find our forks.

The curtains parted. The dancers came out wearing elaborate feather headdresses and long feathered capes. Beautiful. The lights were colorful, panning around the room showcasing the various outfits. The dancers' backs were to us, so we could see the glorious flowing capes and the long trailing headdresses. Slowly, as a group, the dancers started moving, their feathers were gliding with the music. The dancers turned around to face the audience.

Yep, we saw some really creative dances with lots of interesting gyrations. And G-strings. Males with stuffed G-strings and females with overflowing tassels that could spin in different directions.

The trip backs to the ship that night was rather quiet. The boys were a bit stiff in their demeanor. Snell was trying really hard not to laugh, and I was speechless. Who knew the bump-and-grind were native dances and gold lame was a traditional native fabric?

Poodle Skirts

I have worked on my high school reunions for the last fifty years. One of my tasks was to contact people to verify information and to let them know about our reunion plans. I left a number of messages asking people to call or email me back.

Today I had a call from one of the meanest people I knew.

You need to know that I was excruciatingly shy in school. I was an only child, and except for my next-door neighbor and best friend Pickle, I spent most of my time with adults. I lacked confidence when I was with my own age group.

Our elementary school contained kindergarten through the seventh grade. Eighth graders, known as sub-freshmen, began high school. I consider middle school is one of the worst inventions in modern education. You take the most hateful, spiteful, vindictive years of childhood development and put them together in one school! But back to my topic, sixth and seventh grades were exceedingly difficult for me, as they are for many kids. The cause of most of this difficulty was one girl. I shall call her Heifer, for that is what she was--- a bullying, controlling leader of the pack of heifer wannabes.

Daddy worked for the Atlanta Police/School Detectives. He worked every dance and ball game he could to make extra money. Mama worked a full-time job selling insurance for a time and later worked for the

Atlanta school system. We didn't have a lot of money, but we didn't have any debts. If they couldn't pay cash for it, they didn't get it. But we lived well, at least in my mind.

This one girl, Heifer, I now realize, was a bully. I didn't tell anyone how she was, but others surely saw her treatment of me and a few others. I guess they were scared of her vicious tongue, too. If I had only known then what I know now about bullies, I would have recognized her insecurities. She had a need to put people down so that she could feel that she was above someone.

I remember one day I had a new skirt. Back then-- way back then- we had poodle skirts. They were black felt and had an applique of a poodle or another animal. These skirts were all the rage. I got one for Christmas. I was so proud of that skirt. It was new. Mama hadn't made it. It was store bought! We were in the seventh grade at Peterson Elementary School. I remember it vividly.

We HAD to play dodgeball. Heifer, my nemesis, was on the outside, and I was in the center. Heifer was always on the outside when I was in the circle. She would get the ball and aim for me. Wham! I was out. Thank God. I never minded being out in dodgeball. That ball hurt when it hit you, and you were always scuffing up your shoes or your knees trying to avoid being slammed with the so-called soft ball.

I was standing on the side lines when she started on me. "I can't believe you would wear that skirt. It is too long. I'd go naked before I wore such an out of style skirt." On and on that witch went about my new skirt.

When I tell you I was shy, I really was. I didn't have a lot of confidence in myself and especially not enough to stand up against Miss Popularity. She had money. She lived in one of the old big houses in East Atlanta. She had a fashionable "store-bought" haircut with a permanent. She was hot stuff.

I wore my long hair usually in a ponytail. Sometimes Daddy would braid it or put in a colorful scarf to match my outfit. Yes, my Daddy did my hair in the mornings. Mama cooked breakfast, and he helped me get that long mess of hair pulled back. I think wearing that pony tail for all those years is why I have an arch in my eyebrows.

Anyway, back to Heifer, Miss Popularity. Somehow, she never ended up in the center of the dodgeball game so I never got the chance to plant that ball up against her skull. I am pretty sure that was my plan back them. Well, maybe not. I really just stood there, red faced, and took her crap. She made me feel awful and I was never again quite as delighted with my new poodle skirt.

I think that was when I really got into clothes and making a personal statement with my wardrobe. I shopped Goodwill and the Salvation Army to find designer things that Mama could "fine tune". Mama made a lot of my clothes. I was in the Rainbow girls, part of the Masons and Eastern Star organizations. My formals all came from one of the thrift stores, and Mama remade them. Sometimes, she dyed them different colors or took the top from one and grafted it onto the bottom of another. They were all perfectly tailored to fit me, and I am forever grateful.

Miss Heifer was in the same Rainbow organization. I became Worthy Advisor—head honcho. She never got above any of the lower stations. When she finally dropped out, I was glad. I did not have a forgiving heart then. I do try now, but back then, she was burned into the hateful side of my brain.

During all the class reunion calls, I came across her name. I had thought about not calling her number. But why not? It has been at least fifty-five years or more since that day on the playground. We are both old women now, and I really don't care what she thinks.

I dialed her number, and she answered. In that phone call, we had a good conversation and laughed about many things, mostly about ourselves. I learned she had become extremely ill. As Bette Davis said, "Old age is not for sissies." I never mentioned her Poodle Skirt rant during the dodgeball game or how I felt toward her, for I am sure she doesn't remember it.

She never saw herself as a bully, but just righteous in her beliefs. All of her viciousness has drained away. I hope. I gave up my resentment of her that I have held for all of these years. She may have been the first true * itch I had ever met, but maybe age has mellowed her. At one time, I would not have spit on her if her coat tail was on fire, and I was the only person with any water. Now, I would extend a hand. I am not saying that I wouldn't check afterwards to be sure that all my rings and fingers were still there, but I turned loose of all that power I had given her more than five decades ago.

We were young. She was strong. I was weak. The situations are reversed now. I never try to make a person feel bad or self-conscious. I know what that is like. Some people never experience being the fall guy in a bullying game. I think it made me stronger. I know it made me less trustful and more self-protective.

When I went away to college, in my clothes that Mama had made, I spent most of the first year in self-protective mode. I operated on the theory that there were heifers everywhere. I kept my barriers up for a long time, but gradually they began to soften. Thank goodness. I learned I could use humor to deal with most anything that came along.

I know what it was like to be on the other side of the popularity fence, and I decided it was time to change my life. I can stand on top of that fence and not have to be on one side or the other. I can be myself. Like it or lump it.

I have a few close friends. I trust them, but I don't really share a lot about myself, even now. I can have a

228

conversation with someone and come away knowing everything there is to know about them, but the other person will know very little about me. Self- protection just stays with you.

Although I don't have to dress in homemade clothes any more, and my jewels do not come from Woolworth's, I still shop a bargain. I don't have to, but I am not paying full price for anything!

Thank you, Heifer, THE Miss Popularity of Peterson Elementary School. You helped me develop into someone who cares about other people, their needs, and their feelings. You made me conscious of how important it is to present yourself cloaked in confidence, not just the latest fashion. You taught me that I have frailties, but I now know how to treat your wounding statements. I consider the source, block it with my shield, and know that I am the person who is confident and caring. You are the one who is wounded and scared and has to use hatefulness to make yourself feel better about yourself.

Is my poodle skirt too long? Who cares?
It doesn't matter how big your house is,
How much money you have,
Or if you wear expensive clothes.
Our graves will be the same size.
Stay humble.

Droopy Drawers

Can someone please explain to me why men, especially young men, want to wear their pants at half-mast? Let's face it, we have all seen underwear before. It isn't that great, even if it says Captain America on it!

I have worked with teenagers for years. I thought I had seen it all. One day while crossing the cafeteria at Central Gwinnett, a male student was walking in front of me. Students were not supposed to wear their pants hanging down on their fannies. As I got closer to him, I planned to talk to him about the rules and suggest that he pull up his pants and keep them place. I was gaining on him, for I wasn't having to carry something in one hand and holding up my drawers with the other as he was.

This young man was about fifteen feet ahead of me as we were approaching the steps. Suddenly, he reached the third or fourth step and boom! His pants fell to the floor. At least his underwear stayed up. His drawers weren't remarkable, but they managed to stay on his skinny behind.

It was so hard not to laugh out loud. I was biting my tongue and trying not to snicker. I honestly was. Maybe a few snickers might have escaped. The poor soul couldn't get his pants up and hold what he was carrying. He couldn't step up to the main floor because his pants were around his ankles. No matter what he did, he was going to stick his fanny out there while he had me bearing down on him. He just looked at me like deer caught in headlights.

All I could do was pray that I didn't giggle in his face, embarrassing him anymore than he already was. I suggested he lay his parcel down and "take care of business." I was not about to get closer than ten feet from this poor, exposed boy.

He finally put the box down, grabbed his pants, and jerked them up. I swear he pulled them up to his Adam's apple, which was quivering in disgrace. Finally, he was suitably attired and had his box in one hand, pants in the other.

We talked about the rules and his decision to break them. I asked him why he liked to wear his pants like that. He said, "It is in fashion, and everybody does it." As a counselor who has spent many years dealing with children who have suffered from peer pressure, adolescent loss of contact with the world, and just plain thoughtlessness, I had to work hard not to go into the peer pressure speech.

I explained to him that the pants at half-mast was a trend set by men with jail time. Wearing pants at half-mast is a method of silently telegraphing an interest in homosexual activity. I didn't go into that with this young man. He was suffering enough. I did explain that when arrested, belts and shoe strings are taken from the prisoners. The reason is to reduce the chances of suicide and garroting of other inmates. When released from jail, your personal items are some of the last things returned to you. A lot of those leaving the jail house don't take time to put on a belt or lace up shoes. They just want to exit the building as fast as possible. Therefore, when they hit freedom, they have to hold their pants up and do the jail house shuffle. (Hint: If you are going to jail wear elastic waist pants and loafers.)

Why does anyone find this style attractive? Sometimes, I think these males think they are doing the New Zealand Doo-Doo bird mating dance. And they are extinct! That has to be the only thing that could possibly be turned on by someone's drawers and/or crack being displayed. Personally, I like seeing a man dressed well, presenting himself not as if he just left jail, but in a self-confident manner.

Michael Caine once said of Cary Grant, "He saved millions of men from being slobs." It is true. Hollywood sets the fashion, and so many of the current glorified stars look like the devil. Hem your pants and if they are so torn up you can see your pockets or underwear, or lack thereof, throw them away.

A few years ago, I helped with a class in public relations. We did a study of how well people performed on various tasks depending on how they represented themselves. Wardrobe was big part of the project. Those dressed in torn and tattered jeans and shirts performed the worse. They sat with poor posture, paid less attention, gave weak answers, and scored lowest on the tests. Those that dressed in nice jeans and shirts did much better. Those in business-like pants and shirts did the best. We used these people later in another group, scoring them on these same items as well as some other criteria. This time, we asked the poorly dressed to come in business attire and vice versa. Same results.

I wish Cary Grant could have an effect on all of us now. We look like a country of slobs. I really would like to see less flesh and more class. Oh, Cary Grant. Where are you?

Vanity Thy Name is Mine

Yep, I did something purely for looks. I said I wouldn't, but I did. It started out innocently, years ago, and I am just now fessin'up.

Before God started highlighting my hair, I had medium dark brunette hair. My skin color is two steps removed from albino, and my eyelashes and eyebrows are blond. I should have been a blond, but I ended up with the Smith-Evans blend of blue eyes, non-tanning lily white skin, and Evans brown hair. If you were born in Mama's family, and you were blond, you had thick hair like her mother's family, the Smiths. If you had brown hair, it was thin, like her daddy's.

I got thick, brown hair, but all the blond accoutrements of the Smiths. I also got short and fat, again the Smith-Evans genes. My daddy's family was all tall; his mother was six feet. That height in women in the late 1880's was rare. The only things I got from Daddy's side of the family were his thick hair, a cowlick, and his Mama's breast size. I suppose the humongous ta-tas would not be bad if I were six inches taller!

Anyway, back to my vanity. I had only four eyebrow hairs, all white. I cut them down the middle to make them look like I had eight. I used a fine artist's paint brush to draw on individual hairs. I have long eyelashes, but they too are pale. Bless Mary Kay's I Love Mascara. And Great Lash's Royal Blue. Neither smear, and they just stay there where mascara belongs. I have since given up the Royal Blue because I think I am too old for it now, but I may get a wild hair and buy some more.

I thought about gluing on pieces of hair where my eyebrows were ghosting. I tried it, but and the hairs didn't stick well and fell into my eyes. Then, I had running eyes and mascara on my chin. Not a pretty sight.

I had met a woman named Marcie who was a counselor at Berkmar High School. She had her eyebrows tattooed on. I scrutinized her. I looked her eyebrows over with a fine tooth comb, which was useless because she didn't have any fur either. She was a natural red head. Her eyebrows were beautiful. They looked natural, and the color was perfect.

I decided to give myself eyebrows. Barbara McClure of Designing Image was the person who had worked miracles on Marcie's eyebrows. Barbara and I had a consultation, and she looked at the way I had been showcasing my artistic talents of camouflage. She removed my artificial brows and checked my bone structure. She told me that I had been doing a good job of using my natural bone formation for where my eyebrows should have been to create the illusion of brows.

We agreed to give me permanent eyebrows. Best thing I ever did. I never left the house without drawing on eyebrows. Now, I can look at myself in the mirror and not see an eyebrow-less possum looking back. My eyes didn't look like little blue dots in my face, anymore. I had a "frame of eyebrows." People without eyebrows look strange. I am sorry, Whoopi Goldberg, but you choose to shave off your eyebrows, and I would have given a king's ransom for some.

LIFE IS HARD SOFTEN IT WITH LAUGHTER

Now, I have eyebrows. They are perfect. Not too dark, just right. If I only put on mascara, I can go out in public and not be too frightening. I am so glad I did it.

Did it hurt? Yeah, little bit. She deadens all the tissue very well before she begins the procedure. You sneeze a lot while she is working on you because the needling is at that nerve point that tingles when you feel a sneeze coming on. The thawing stage is a bit strange feeling. It took three sessions to get my eyebrows completely done. Would I get another tattoo? Not on your life. I have three blue dots from radiation therapy, and I didn't want them.

But my eyebrows were worth the pain

When Hell Froze Over

We have had such beautiful spring weather recently. The temperatures have been in the 70's and low 80's. The pollen count has been in the thousands. There has been just enough light rain to wash some of the pollen out and allow the beautiful colors to shine through.

There was a significant drop in the temperatures today. The high has hovered around 61 degrees and below. "So, it's spring," you say. "The temperatures do vary oddly at this time of year". HA. This isn't the cause.

Hell froze over.

Every time there is a significant drop in the temperature, it is because Hell is beginning to freeze over. Women the world over tell themselves they are free of certain terrible experiences, such as panty hose. Then something happens. They are forced into a dress and panty hose. Temperatures start to drop because she said at one time, "Hell will freeze over before I ever do this again."

Today was my day. I controlled the temperatures of Hell. I had esophageal repair surgery and as a result have lost something like forty pounds. Because of the constant change in my weight, clothes shopping has been a futile effort. The one thing lacking in my wardrobe was a nice pair of "funeral britches."

I was raised to dress and look your best. Even if your clothes are not expensive, you better be clean, neat, and dressed appropriately. Mama always left for work dressed to the nines. She was so happy when Jackie Kennedy introduced the pants suit, and it became an acceptable clothing choice for all occasions. Mama told me not to wear black or a dress with panty hose to her funeral, and, "For God's sake, don't put me in a dress or hose. I am going free through the gates of Heaven." For her funeral, Mama wore pink socks with butterflies, white pants and a pink blouse. I knew she had meant what she said and she would haunt me if I did not respect her final wishes.

Jeans are not appropriate for funerals. Neither are sloppy t-shirts. And horizontal patterns on fat girls are never appropriate for any occasion. Dress to impress. Dress for success. How about just dressing to be respectful and respectable?

My wardrobe was limited. I only had "messing around" clothes. Granted I try to look nice for messing around, but not funeral nice.

When I retired from Parkview High school in 2002, I swore I would never wear a dress or panty hose ever again. The chilling temperatures of Hell graced my world on this day. Snell and I were going to a funeral. I tried on every nice pair of pants I had. My standard funeral suit pants fell to my ankles while I was wearing them. Desperation was an understatement to my fashion dilemma. My one hope for salvation was the storage closet upstairs. There had to be something there. There was....

A black sheathe dress with a dark purple pattern on it hung forlornly in the closet. I heaved it over my head and it hung on my body. A black sweater helped to camouflage my upper arms. They have not seen the light of day since I was thirty-two and a size twelve. I looked like a bag lady in clothes made for someone three sizes larger, but I was covered.

The next step was shoes and stockings. The dress had a slit. I couldn't get by with knee highs. I haven't bought panty hose in fourteen years. Knee high stockings were raining across our bed from being plucked from my unmentionable's drawer. I spied one long pantyhose leg AND it was black. The next hurdle was the struggle to pull them on. At one point I got my left leg in the right foot and nearly flipped myself out the window. I managed to pull those suckers on. For those of you who have never worn pantyhose, "suckers" is the right word. They suck you in on the bottom half and puff you out on the top. The industrial strength elastic in those pantyhose was still sucking!!! Fourteen years and the elastic was still good. I had been expecting to have to resort to duct tape and staples.

I slid on my little heels and looked in the mirror. EEK. The best I could say was that I was wearing clothes. I wouldn't be upset if my husband didn't sit with me and the rest of his family didn't acknowledge my presence.

People were nice, I think. Many commented, "I understand you have been sick." Or "Have you been ill?" I loved the dear little old lady who looked at me and said, "Honey, I had that same dress some twenty years ago. It doesn't look really good on you either. "

I must have looked worse than the gal in the box, and the temperature had dropped to 54.

Travel Cooties

I am never going on another trip. Every time we go somewhere, I get sick. I get a false sense of security on a trip. I am having a nice time. All is good. But lurking in the shadows is the sicky-ickies.

Yep, THE dreaded sicky-ickies. They exist. We called them germs and viruses, but they are cooties, and they are out to get me. The sicky-ickies are worse than average cooties. They can take down a water buffalo with a single puff of breath. I know. I am the size of a water buffalo, and, trust me, they took me down. HARD.

We returned from our vacation, and I began the long arduous task of laundry and re-establishing relations with the Flying Monkeys (cats). By the end of the second day, I was sneezing. Did you know you kill brain cells every time you sneeze? You really do. That is going to be my answer when someone asks me what's wrong or why I can't find something. Like my niece's Christmas present that I put up while we were gone. It took me three days to find it.

On the third day, I couldn't swallow. Of course, it was the weekend, and the doctor's office was closed. What? You think I could get sick on a normal schedule? Get real. I went to an urgent care facility. With my health issues, I knew I had to get on an antibiotic pretty quickly.

The physician's assistant was delightful. Cute little twelve-year olds running the office. The combined age of the entire urgent care people may have been 28. How

239

did the world get so young? And if you say, "Maybe it is because you got so old," I swear I will find you and breathe,   sneeze, and cough on you. I am a deadly weapon.

The physician's assistant said she thought I had a virus and not a bacterial infection. I told her I wanted Keflex in large quantities, no matter what it was. I also wanted cough medicine and an iron lung. She just smiled.

I guess this was a virus because the antibiotics were not touching it. I looked like a raccoon with red instead of black eyes, and surely, I was dehydrated from all the snot I had produced. The thought to give up on Kleenex and just tie a plastic bag around my waist and hang a roll of toilet paper around my neck was entertained.

Snort, cough, sneeze, sigh.

Express Yourself

I adore funny t-shirts. I really do. I don't wear them. Short, fat, little old ladies are not that appealing in cute t-shirts. We tend to give others the right to create their own 'funny" reactions to us. "Did you see that old woman wearing the "I am a Princess" T-shirt? She looks like an old faded queen."

Have you ever thought about how big someone's chest must be to fit some of those slogans on it? It would be impressive. Frightening, maybe, but still impressive.

One of my favorites is "I just did a week's worth of cardio after walking into a spider web." It is true. I can hit a spider web and levitate four feet into the air, all the while doing my spider scream. Mama had an "I walked into a worm" scream. I have perfected mine for spiders and their webs. Snell and James don't even respond. I heard James tell his Daddy one day after I had a close encounter of the near fatal kind with a spider, "Mom just saw a spider." They didn't even check on me. Nor did they come to kill the beast which was at least the size of a dinner plate. Maybe a little smaller. He lived only because I ran the other way.

Another one I love is "Nurses—We can't fix stupid, but we can sedate it." Isn't it the truth? Don't you wish you had a syringe full of happy juice when someone acts like a fool around you? Snell and I were in the grocery store line the other day, and a little old lady was checking out. Her grandson was with her and he was trying to help. He just made things worse.

241

She was becoming addled. Someone had given her a gift card and she didn't know how much was on it or how to use it. The cashier was telling her to slide it in the credit card machine. I don't think she had ever used a credit card machine. The more people helped, the more confused she became. It is what it is, and we just waited on her. No sense in getting upset. However, the dufus behind us in line was acting all huffy-puffy because it was taking so long.

I really wanted to slap the stuffing out of him. If I had a syringe of happy juice, he surely would have gotten it. Instead, I gave him my sweetest (those are the most venomous) smiles and told him if this was causing him problems to go to another line. I also said, "Do you help your mother shop?" He glared at me. Hey, I taught school for over thirty-four years. A glare bounces off me. I gave him my Mama's "The Look," and he shut up. He didn't move, but he didn't huff, puff, or snarl anymore. AND the woman's grandson thanked me for being so patient with her. So, did the cashier. Bet the dufus didn't get a thank you. He should have gotten a syringe.

Speaking of "The Look," I was never spanked. "The Look" took care of everything. Here is a shirt that I need "Sometimes when I open my mouth my mother comes out..." Or "Don't give me trouble, I know The Look." Have you ever looked down and saw your mother's hands? I did that the other day, and thought I am becoming my mama. I have her hands, The Look, and I am using the same old expressions—time takes care of all things. Oh, and I tell stories from long ago.

And here is another goodie that I think I will have printed on my business cards: "If I give you straw, will you suck the fun out of someone else's' day?" You all know you want to do it, too.

"Danger. Do not approach. Eye contact can cause fatality" Wear that when you are having one of those days. The first fool who approaches will be eyebrowless. I have wanted the snatch the eyebrows off a lot of people in my lifetime.

"Warning. Baldness is not a genetic condition. It occurs when you irritate me."

I want a shirt that says, "When I say so!" so all I have to do it point to my chest.

Of course, there is the shirt that only buxom women should wear: "Things in the rear- view mirror ARE larger than they appear."

MARLENE RATLEDGE BUCHANAN

Southern Musings

One thing I would like to say to all the people we are trying to save by allowing them to move south is this: You can make fun of us. You can think we are ignorant, but the fact of the matter is *YOU* chose to move here. And, I don't have an accent. Y'all do.

My First Day

Not sure why but Roosevelt High School in Atlanta was on my mind this morning. That was where I started my "formal" teaching career. My "informal" career began at the age of nine, teaching swimming lessons at Misty Waters. But Roosevelt High School was big time. And I got a pay check for more than $6.00 a week.

The City of Atlanta hired me to teach art classes in summer school and assigned me to Roosevelt. Roosevelt was the Grant Park (AKA Zoo Atlanta) side of East Atlanta, where I lived. There was a possibility I would get to remain in the fall. The teacher who normally taught had been ill and had surgery. There was a chance she was going to have to take early retirement.

I was on the second floor and had two huge classrooms, both with sinks and running water. There was an office/storage room with a telephone. One room had kick wheels and two kilns for clay work. The art supplies consisted of watercolors, conte pencils, tempera paints galore, and all kinds of appropriate paper. I had hit the motherlode for art teachers.

I proudly wrote the schedule on the chalk board and printed my name: Marlene Ratledge. I was a teacher! I smiled and knew I had a promising career ahead of me.

The first class ambled in and finally got settled. I introduced myself and started explaining that this was an art class that was going to focus on drawing, color and painting. Twenty-one students comprised the first period.

A thin ebony arm went up in the back of the classroom while I passed out a form for each student to complete. "Yes Sir. Tell me your name and what can I do for you." (I later learned to never ask teenage boys what I could do for them.)

"Is you any kin to that po-liceman, Detective Ratledge?"

I was so proud. "Yes, I am. He is my daddy."

"He arrested me."

Someone else raised his hand, and said "Yeah, he arrested me, too."

Gulp. I smiled. "Oh, I'm sorry." I'm sorry? Wait a minute! I'M sorry??? I didn't do anything. YOU did something. I was preparing for the worst.

Daddy, who was a City of Atlanta School Detective, had arrested twelve of my students from my first period class. As the day went on, I met other students who also had contact with Daddy. During the summer, students would stop by and introduce themselves. Daddy had helped a girl who was assaulted. She came from another classroom to tell me how kind he had been and how he had caught the man who did it. Others stopped by and just said they knew him.

If Daddy and/or J. D. Hudson, one of Daddy's most respected partners and friends, were working a case nearby, they would stop in. Daddy was over 6'4" and had snow white hair. J.D. was his matching image, except he was black and his hair was greying, not quite snow white. They were an imposing sight walking down the hall.

Daddy, J.D., other school detectives, and several uniformed officers knew I had a phone, and they could use it without having to displace someone in the front office. It got to where the kids didn't even blink to hear, "Patsy, can I use the office?" (Patsy? That's me, Patricia Marlene.) I would toss them the keys and continue our class.

The kids were wonderful. I think of them often and wonder about them. There was the scam artist that I know has had to do jail time for theft and receiving stolen goods. He had a monkey and would come back after school with the monkey to show him off. And Daisy, who drew a cartoon and gave it to me. It was about being pregnant. That is how she told me she was going to have a baby. And my little Jeffery, who had announced that Daddy had arrested him at the start of that first period so many years ago. He was one of my favorites. He would come back after school and help me clean up the room, and I would drop him off at his house. I got to meet his grandmother and his older sisters. His grandmother made the best chocolate pound cake. I visited with them several times and kept in touch for a while after I was shipped to Hoke Smith High School on Hill Street. It was located right behind the original Atlanta Stadium.

I had one room on the third floor of Hoke Smith, and mine was the only classroom in use. There was no one up there but me and my kids. I was told bluntly by the principal, "I am only hiring you because I know your dad, and you are white." This was a different world. The Roosevelt kids had been delightful. They had come in and had a good time in class and were a joy. The Hoke Smith kids came in sullen and challenging. It wasn't race. I had just as many black kids at Roosevelt. It was a neighborhood attitude.

Conversations with them were stilted. I felt like any observation I made was taken as a challenge. Any kind words were treated with mistrust. In the third week, I was there two girls came running into my classroom. One had been slapped in the face and a boy had tried to rape her. Crying, she told me of how she had fought and how he had tried to throw her off the roof. The second girl heard the yelling. She had helped the first girl to get away. They had slipped up to the roof to smoke. I went with them down to the main office and stayed with them until the school detective and their parents got there. I was dismissed and went back to my class. Word had gotten around that I had been able to identify the boy. I had not seen him and really knew nothing more than his first name, which the girls had told me.

The next day I was standing at the doorway to my classroom. Homeroom had been dismissed, and first period students were on the way. A young man with one white eye that looked like it had a thick cataract-like scar tissue over it came up and told me that I "didn't know nothing." He was menacing, and I was scared of him. He put his hands on me inappropriately and was gone in just a flash. I reported it, but nothing came of it. He was older and not a student.

That day, a female student took a pair of scissors and jammed them into my thigh. Thank goodness my skirt was thick enough to deflect the blades, but I ended up with a nice bruise.

I went home that night and told my parents about my day and that I had reported it all. The next morning, I got up to reluctantly go to work. Mama and Daddy told me to take the day off and go back to West Georgia to find out about graduate school. That was the first time in my life I ever missed a day of work. I had graduated from elementary through high school and all of college and never missed a single day of school. Eighteen years of perfect attendance, and I was told to play hooky that day. It was not in our genetic make-up to not do our job.

I was accepted into Graduate School that day and returned the next morning to tender my resignation. I worked four days before a replacement was found. I always regretted that I was not successful at Hoke Smith.

A year later, I went to Duluth High School. I wrote my name on the board and promptly became "Miss Rat" to most of my students. Bob Jones started calling me "Art Woman." This was another first day and kicked off a thirty-four-year teaching career.

Every day is a first day for something. I hope your first days will always be good ones.

Three on a Match

I have always heard that bad things happen in threes. I think the expression began with World War I and the prohibition for a third person to light a cigarette on one match. Never three on a match. In the amount of time it takes for three people to light their cigarettes, the enemy can find and focus on them and, "Boom," they would be dead.

Mama and Daddy would say things like, "That's two. Wonder what number three is." All of my life, I have counted bad things in threes. I hope we have had our three bad luck things.

Our son James had some medication changes and had a reaction to them. He can't take decongestants and some other medications because they give him tics, uncontrollable muscle spasms. He had been on the same medications for almost fifteen years though, so the doctor thought we needed to reduce one of them that has the greatest side effects. In the process of reducing one and adding another, James started having the St. Vitus Dance symptoms again. That's one.

Then he got the flu. And because he loves us, he shared the flu with his daddy and me. And the flu was really bad. I thought I had lost Snell to the great light at the end of the tunnel one night. That's two.

And because three people with the flu, (one near death), plus a sick cat (another story for another time) aren't enough pleasures in one household----I set the kitchen on fire. Big flames. Real flames. Lots of black oily smoke from burning plastic.

Burning plastic stinks. Once the fire was out, we turned on the attic fan, lit candles, and started washing things in vinegar, soap, and water. The smoke and the fire extinguisher matter had coated everything including our lungs. We were all coughing worse because we were still sick with the flu. We may be lucky that we had all this phlegm in our lungs already. Maybe it caught some of the smoke because what we coughed up was flecked with black debris. Appetizing, isn't it? Sorry, but true.

No one was hurt, except that I got a couple of burns on my leg. The source of the fire was a pan with a plastic lid in the drawer under the oven. The lid caught fire. I put the fire out, but when I was trying to throw the pan of hot plastic outside, the boiling liquid splattered on my shin. It just resulted in tiny little burns, but one was kind of deep. I managed to peel the hot plastic off and debrided the burn site, but ouch!

Anyway, all the smoke alarms work, so the Gwinnett Emergency Service called and asked if I needed a fire truck. I started to tell her only if it was filled with ice cream or liquor.

I cleaned the stove for two days. I should have called the insurance people, but no, I started cleaning. The drawer under the oven was coated in melted plastic. The instructions on this oven were to soak spills with plain water and wipe with a cloth. That was doing the trick inside the oven, but the plastic had to be chiseled with a plastic knife.

The furniture in the dining and living rooms was covered in sheets because of the cats. They think that is their room, so they like everything to be covered in cat hair. The washing machine and dryer were running almost constantly as we washed everything in the house. The burnt plastic odor had disappeared, but it took some time and a lot of effort.

LIFE IS HARD SOFTEN IT WITH LAUGHTER

Every year, I tackle the house one room at a time and clean it thoroughly. I decided after all this to move my cleaning schedule ahead and begin immediately. I move through the house, polishing the furniture, cleaning and washing all the knick-knacks, curtains, etc. So far this year, the kitchen, den, dining and living rooms are complete. I have the bedroom to face next. I didn't realize how much crap I have.

This house will soon be so clean. You have to come see it before the spiders can move back in and the cats shed another fourteen pounds of hair.

Now, here is proof that the flu burned out all of my sensible brain cells. As I said, I did not call the insurance company. We have been cleaning furiously. I am an old, fat woman who has been lying on her back, wiping soot from this stove and trying to chisel melted plastic from under the oven.

Finally, Snell said, "This stove is twenty-two years old. We can afford to buy a new one. Why are we doing this?"

I got up (eventually) and said, "I'll order a new one in the morning."

What in the world was I thinking, trying to clean this stove like this? Why was I was determined to save this old stove? And for what? It has been established I am not a domestic diva, and my three types of meals consist of take-out, delivery, or reservations. I certainly had no emotional attachment to it. It's sort of like my uterus. Used once, don't need it anymore.

Please, let that be number three.

Southern Speak

D o we speak differently in the South? Yes, we do. And we speak differently in various regions of the South. That Virginia drawl is nothing compared to a true Georgia one.

And some of the words we use have a different pronunciation and meaning than in other places in the world. There are some Southern words that are just hard for some people to understand. Well, part of it is those people who are not used to listening to our drawl and part of it is our way defining things. Our language is a bit more colorful and descriptive than some other parts of the USA.

Many times, when I would be enrolling a new student and the family into the school system, someone would comment on my "accent." I would just look at them and in my most pitying smile I would tell them "Honey, here I DON'T have an accent...YOU do." Eventually, I would let them know we saved another one by letting 'em move South.

It was necessary to teach these new comers important things. Y'all is a contraction YOU plus ALL. The apostrophe is because you have dropped the letters "ou" and made a contraction. (Basic Southern grammar.) A COKE is any carbonated drink. A CO-COLA is a Coca Cola. A POP is someone's father or grandfather or a special older male friend. A SODA is sody water, a mixture of baking soda and water for indigestion. HEY is a greeting. HAY is used for animal fodder.

We are frequently FIXIN' to do something. That means we are about to start a project. We are "fixin' to go" to the store means in a few minutes we will be leaving the house to go shopping. "I might need to run to town." "I might not need to leave." Might means another decision has to be made before a definitive answer can be given. How hard is that?

My next-door neighbors' little boy was in our yard one day. His pants were too big and kept falling half way to the ground. I said "Louie, let me pull up your britches." His mother asked me what "britches" were. I swear to goodness.

We swear some too. "I swear to goodness." "I swear I have never seen anything like it." "I swear it is a beautiful day." "I swear I am going get you for that." "I swear that was the biggest dang spider I ever saw." We are not being disrespectful to anyone or anything. We are simply declaring that that particular thing was impressive. Good or bad, it was impressive.

Although times have changed some have not. Many of us still eat breakfast, dinner, and supper. And we tend to eat supper all together at the same table. Lunch is one of those words that has made it into the Southern vocabulary. But it was a true Southern lady who created "lupper." Lupper is the meal that falls between lunch and supper. Some of you would call it a late lunch or an early supper.

I might be telling you all some things you already know, but it is time you learned them if you don't. You can make fun us and the slower way we talk and our colloquialisms (See, we even know big words.) all you want. The truth is, the old Southern expressions are fading because so many people from other parts of the world have moved here. It is a shame, but it is true.

We address older people as Miss Teena or Mr. Vernon. They are older and had many more experiences that we. They deserve a little title of respect. We tend to say "Yes, ma'am" and "No, sir." Again, it shows respect, and the Southern culture was very respectful of elders as well as people in positions of authority.

We might shoot you for doing something wrong, but we surely did respect you, and you will get a decent send-off to the after-life, whether it is heaven or hell.

One thing I would like to say to all the people we are trying to save by allowing them to move south is this: You can make fun of us. You can think we are ignorant, but the fact of the matter is YOU chose to move here. If you don't think the south is as close to Heaven as you can get without taking your last breath, go back from whence you came. We like it here. If you don't, we won't force you to stay. And we will respect your decision to leave.

Well, I swear to all y'all. It is time for me to pull up my britches and head back home. I think there might be some red-eye gravy and cornbread waiting on me for supper. It's been good talking to you. Y'all take care now and come see us when you can. In the meantime, laugh a little because life is hard and should be softened with laughter.

Marlene

Acknowledgements

Several people need to be recognized for their support, encouragement, and literary skills. Without them, this endeavor would never have made it to print.

Cecelia Landress: Cece kept after me to do write this book. She dragged me to classes and encouraged me to keep writing. No matter how bad something was written, she found a positive in it.

Auveed Cawthon: The Editor of the Gwinnett Citizen offered me the opportunity to write for the monthly local newspaper. Many of these essays started out as short pieces she printed.

Chesta Drake: Words are just not enough to thank Chesta. She taught English and Language Arts and then became a counselor. She first worked with Snell. After retirement, she and I worked together for five years. She has read every word many times. She held my hand through the writing process and offered her shoulder, a box of Kleenex, and a great deal of giggles and laughter. Whatever was needed, Chesta was there. A great editor, a dear friend, with her this book would never have made it to fruition.

MARLENE RATLEDGE BUCHANAN

LIFE IS HARD SOFTEN IT WITH LAUGHTER

About the Author

Marlene is the author of the southern humor column, Hey Y'all. The column began as blog on the Snellville Patch and is now a featured column in the monthly newspaper, The Gwinnett Citizen.

With over 34 years of teaching and counseling in high schools, she is more than well versed in adolescent hormone and parent nightmares. Her students called her Ms. Rat and through the years she has been gifted with a significant collection of mice/rats and other rodent-like vermin.

She married her husband 364 days after their first date. Marlene is quick to tell anyone she wanted a rich old man. She only got old, but Snell has made her life so much richer. Together, they have one child, now a grown man, who is mildly mentally handicapped and is a blessing—often in disguise.

Connect with Marlene

Facebook: @marleneratledgebuchanan

Web: msratwrites.com

Email: msratwrites@gmail.com

Goodreads: MarleneRatledgeBuchanan

The best way to thank an author is to leave a review. Please share how much you enjoyed Marlene's book with other readers.

MARLENE RATLEDGE BUCHANAN

52059110R10150

Made in the USA
Columbia, SC
02 March 2019